(Above) A general view of the Westgate and St Dunstan's areas. Of special note are the extensive greenhouses of George Mount & Sons in Forty Acres Road (top of the picture), and the 'new' houses on the opposite side of the road. Also of interest are the many lost buildings along North Lane and on either side of the railway crossing in St Dunstan's Street.

(Kentish Gazette)

(Below) The West Station and its extensive coal and goods yard. It seems a hive of activity, compared with the derelict wasteland we find there today. Note the Canterbury and Whitstable Railway branching off to the north, complete with departing train, climbing towards Tyler Hill Tunnel. The many allotments along the south side of Roper Road are also things of the past.

(Kentish Gazette)

ST DUNSTAN'S STREET

This fascinating wintry picture of St Dunstan's Street was taken before the First World War from the railway crossing and looks towards the Westgate Towers.

Many surviving late medieval timber framed buildings can be seen along the street's south side in both the old and current photographs. Nearest the camera on the right is the triple gabled House of Agnes, which is thought to be the one described by Charles Dickens, in 'David Copperfield', as belonging to Mr Wickfield. By the late 1930s it had become a café run by Mesdames Wells, Smith and Williams.

Further down on the same side, and opposite the junction with Station Road West, can be found another medieval triple gabled building, which had at one time been the Star Inn. By the time the old picture was taken the inn had long gone, and the building divided into three parts as Nos. 77 to 79 St Dunstan's Street. By the late 1930s it was still three separate parts; a private dwelling, a grocer's and draper's shop respectively.

A number of buildings on the other side of St Dunstan's Street were destroyed in the blitz of Canterbury, including some that can be seen on the left of the old photograph. The south side received considerable blast damage, particularly the former Star Inn, but fortunately was not beyond repair and restoration.

Today, the south side of St Dunstan's Street has altered little since the early years of this century, and only the occupants have changed. The House of Agnes is now a restaurant and hotel, and two thirds of the old Star Inn have been reunited as a hospice shop. The other third has become an extension for the Rose and Crown public house next door.

(Fisk-Moore)

Many of the pilgrims to Canterbury would have approached the city along the London Road. Having reached St Dunstan's Church, a right turn would have brought the traveller into St Dunstan's Street, as it would today. The gateway into the city known as the Westgate is now only a few hundred yards away.

This picture dates from around 1939 and shows traffic queuing up at the level crossing in St Dunstan's Street. Many of the buildings visible on the left of the street would be lost in the blitz of Canterbury. Partially hidden behind the lorry is a row of four cottages known as Railway Buildings, and nearer the crossing is the larger house at No. 28 St Dunstan's Street; the premises of the antique dealer Ernest Lee. The tallest of the buildings beyond the crossing would also be lost, as described in the caption below.

(Kent Messenger)

This superb photograph was taken from the top of the Westgate in the late 1920s, and looks back along St Dunstan's Street. Motor vehicles are already much in evidence, including a single-deck bus at the far end. The tiled pitched roofs in the foreground belong to the buildings that can be seen at ground level in the bottom picture. The impressive range of three storey shop buildings on the far side of Station Road West can be clearly seen from this high vantage point. They became victims of the bombing as did the partially hidden buildings on the opposite side of the road. However, they were probably not the intended target of the Luftwaffe, who were more likely aiming for the extensive railway coal and goods yard, only a few yards to the right.

(Fisk-Moore)

This lovely St Dunstan's Street scene was captured in the 1920s. It was taken from the level crossing and looks towards the Westgate. The many and varied buildings on the north side of the street, most of them medieval and timber framed, can be seen on the left of the picture. The most famous of these is undoubtedly the Falstaff Inn that proudly claims to have been established in 1403. Another inn of medieval origin is the nearby George and Dragon (now called The Bishop's Finger). The two buildings nearest the camera, and next to the junction with Kirbys Lane, were victims of the Second World War. The timber framed shop was the premises of Charles Savery the baker, and the brick building right on the junction was the tobacconist shop of George Wheatley.

(Fisk-Moore)

THE WESTGATE AREA

This dramatic old cityscape was taken from the top of the Westgate towers around 1935. This date, although not certain, is probable as the view includes the Friars Cinema (now the new Marlowe Theatre) which was opened in 1933. The picture also includes a Barretts building destroyed by fire in 1937. It is the one second away from the camera, and was later replaced by a modern 'art deco' influenced garage building. Unfortunately, the vast majority of the Barretts complex was destroyed in an isolated incendiary attack in 1944. In recent years Barretts have been allowed to redevelop their site, but only after the plans to complete the ring road had been dropped.

In the old photograph the tower of the Victorian All Saints' Church can just be made out halfway up the main street. It stood on the corner of the High Street with Best Lane, and was demolished as redundant in 1938. Another lost church is the Congregational Church in Guildhall Street, whose grey tiled roof can be seen dead centre of the 1935 view. This church was partially demolished around 1948, and the remains converted into an extension to Lefevres Stores. Also just visible at the far end of the main street is the spire on top of St George's Parish Church.

The mature trees to the right of the Cathedral are 'The Oaks' in the south east corner of the precincts. Most of these old trees were felled in 1949, just prior to the post-war redevelopment of the blitzed areas of the precinct and the north side of Burgate Street.

It is perhaps reassuring that there are more similarities than differences between the two views, especially the Cathedral which dominates the cityscape both then and now.

(Kent Messenger)

Sudbury Tower is one of three city wall bastions which have survived along Pound Lane. It was built at the same time as the Westgate, and is named after the archbishop of the time. Simon Sudbury contributed towards the cost of the rebuilding of the city defences in this area. Unfortunately Archbishop Sudbury was brutally murdered in the Peasants Revolt, whilst this work was still in progress. The photograph was taken in the early 1900s, at about the time when the building had been condemned as unsafe.

Fortunately, Sudbury Tower was subsequently saved and beautifully restored. The brick chimney and hipped roof were removed, and the tower rebuilt to its original height. Today, the benevolent ghost of Simon Sudbury is said to haunt this old bastion which carries his name.

(H.B. Collis)

280. Sudbury Tower. Canterbury.

After 1380, all pilgrims to Canterbury who arrived by the London Road would have needed to pass between the impressive drum towers of the Westgate. The gate, with its many defensive features including draw-bridge, battlements and gunloops, was built in troubled times. England faced danger not only from France, but from its own people (the Peasants Revolt occurred in 1381).

This picture was taken in 1941, in more recent troubled times, and shows the Westgate during one of the many fundraising weeks of that year, held to encourage the purchase of war bonds. These events included war weapons week, the Spitfire fund, tank week and the many salvage schemes. The wartime look-out post can be seen atop the northern drum tower.

Westgate is the only city gate to have survived intact, although remains of Wincheap Gate can also still be found.

(Fisk-Moore)

North Lane runs approximately parallel to Pound Lane, but is on the outside of the line of the city wall. The lane had been fully developed on both sides in medieval times, and some of these ancient buildings can still be seen today. However, the old cottage in the photograph is not medieval, nor has it survived. In fact it was one of the two tiny cottages in Canterbury claiming to be the 'umble 'ome of Uriah Heep from 'David Copperfield'. Charles Dickens is thought to have written this famous novel in Canterbury, and describes a number of the city's buildings therein. The other claimant to the title was on the other side of Canterbury in Lower Chantry Lane (see page 49). Unfortunately, both of Uriah Heep's cottages were destroyed in the blitz of Canterbury. The site of this particular building in North Lane is now a surface car park.

(H.B. Collis)

5

ST PETER'S PLACE

It would be easy to get the impression from the many 'Then and Now' articles features so far, that most of Canterbury has changed beyond all recognition in the last 50 years. This is not the case, and much of Canterbury in areas unaffected by the blitz and 1960s planners has remained largely unaltered for many decades, if not many centuries!

Although 90 years separates the two photographs shown here, the changes are not considerable. The most obvious change is the disappearance of the corner house on the left of the picture at No. 33 St Peter's Street. At the time the old picture was taken it was the photographic shop and studio of H.B. Collis, who took many views of Canterbury in the early years of the century, including this photograph. By the 1920s it had received stucco plasterwork and other embellishments, and had become the Corner House Café. The East Kent Road Car Company also had their traffic offices in the building. By the late 1930s the café had given way to the showrooms of the City and County Borough of Canter-

bury Electricity Department. After the war it reverted to being a photographic shop, before being demolished in 1961 to make way for a ring road that never came.

The Church of the Holy Cross was built around 1380, in the decorated and perpendicular Gothic styles, and has changed very little over the centuries. However, the tower was rebuilt in the 1880s to reduce both its height and bulk.

The only difference between the old and current views here is the absence of the old iron railings, which were removed in 1941 to aid the war effort.

The Westgate Towers have also changed little over the years, thank goodness! It is just a shame that none of the other city gates have survived.

(H.B. Collis)

This Cafe is the most up-to-date in the City, and is fitted with the only

American Soda Fountain in Canterbury.

"Every Convenience,"

It is renowned for pure Cream Ices, Sundaes, Parfaits, Ice Cream Sodas, etc.

Catering in all its branches, Ballroom, Receptions, Banquets, etc.

Distance no object.

Another view of the corner house, this time taken from the archway of the Westgate. It dates from around 1940, by which time the corner house and adjacent building in St Peter's Street had become an electricity showroom. An East Kent coach departs from the St Peter's Place Bus Station for Deal, having travelled in on the London Express Service. The vehicle is a Leyland TS8 coach from 1938 and is one of a batch of 50 similar coaches. They seated 32 persons and lasted well into the 1950s. As mentioned opposite, the corner house and adjacent building were demolished in 1961. Earlier, in 1956, the St Peter's Place Bus Station relocated to St George's Lane where it can be found today. However, since the ring road plans were dropped, rebuilding of the corner house has been mooted several times, but no definite plans have yet surfaced.

(Bill Entwistle)

St Peter's Place is one of three parallel roads coming off St Peter's Street that were largely created and developed for housing in the nineteenth century. The other two are Black Griffin Lane and St Peter's Grove. The whole development was built on open land within the city walls, much of which used to belong to the Franciscan order of the Grey Friars. The old photograph was taken in the late 1930s from just beyond the Bus Station, and looks up St Peter's Place. This particular area was threatened with virtual extinction by the post war planners. St Peter's Place would have disappeared to make way for the ring road, but the plans were severely curtailed.

However, the road was linked into the new Rheims Way in 1963, and the front gardens swept away to widen the road in readiness for all the new through traffic.

(Kent Messenger)

As mentioned on page 5, three defensive bastions from the old city wall can still be found along Pound Lane. A fourth square-shaped bastion can also be seen in the Westgate Gardens, and survives today as part of Tower House. The main part of Tower House was built onto the bastion, probably in the early 17th century, as it shows a Jacobean influence, popular at this time. Then, around 1870, the two Victorian wings were added. It is in this extended state that Tower House is pictured here, probably in the 1920s, whilst still a private residence, owned by the Williamson family.

In 1936 the eleven acres of gardens and Tower House itself were given to the city, and the Westgate Public Gardens came into being. It was at around this time that the two Victorian wings were demolished and public seating areas created in their place.

(Kent Messenger)

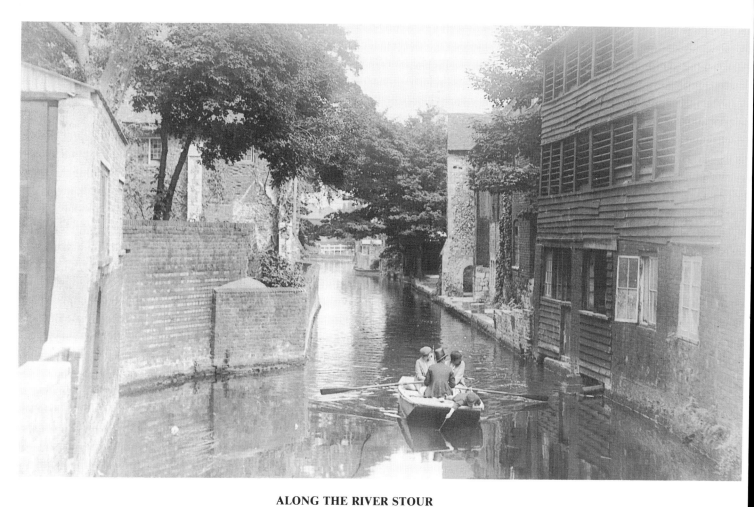

ALONG THE RIVER STOUR

The old photograph dates from July 1932 and was taken from the Friars bridge, looking north along the River Stour. The name The Friars comes from the dominican Blackfriars, who once had a friary covering much of this area. The friary was founded in 1230 and dissolved in the Reformation. Two buildings from the old friary have survived, one on each side of the river, and can be seen in both pictures. The building on the left is the old Blackfriars guest hall, and surviving on the opposite bank of the river is the former refectory block. This refectory building had been 'restored' in the 1920s and, at the time of the old photograph, was being used by the Unitarian Church.

The building in the foreground on the left is part of the premises of Friars Garage Ltd. In the centre of the picture, and about to pass beneath the photographer, is the Blackfriars ferry-boat which once plied its trade along this stretch of the River Stour.

The large wooden structure to the right of the picture belonged to Green and Company — Fellmongers, and is built on what was once part of the Blackfriars churchyard. Incidentally, a fellmonger is one who prepares animal skins for the tanner. Their curious three storey premises were probably a victim of the blitz, but in any event had definitely gone by the late 1940s. The Friends Meeting House now occupies the site, and can partly be seen in the current view.

In recent years both surviving buildings of the old Blackfriars have been more carefully restored. The old guest hall is regularly used for concerts, exhibitions and other social events, whilst the refectory building is now an arts centre for the King's School.

(Fisk-Moore)

The photographs on the opposite page were taken from the Friars Bridge looking north. This is a southerly view from the same bridge and was taken in the 1920s. The scene has undergone a number of changes, but none were caused by the blitz of Canterbury. The tower of the Victorian All Saints' Church can just be made out in the background, although its image is largely burnt out by the sunlight. However, the church tower is casting a strong shadow in the calm waters of the River Stour, and this can clearly be seen. All Saints' became redundant and was pulled down in the late 1930s. A number of the decrepit-looking riverside warehouses on the left were demolished in the 1950s. However, the more substantial dwelling house on the right, known as Friars Cottage, still survives.

No book on old Canterbury is complete without a picture of the 1909 Floods, and this one is no exception. The photograph was taken in November of that year from the end of Pound Lane. It looks across the junction of The Causeway to the left, and into a crowded St Radigund's Street in the distance. The Tower Inn is on the left of the picture standing at the junction with The Causeway. The pub was named as such because it adjoined an old square-shaped bastion from the city wall, which had been converted into a house. Later, the Tower Inn became a hairdressers' shop before being demolished in the 1960s.

Flooding has occurred on a number of occasions since 1909, most recently in January 1988, when the force of the flood water caused damage to bridges and riverside retaining walls in this vicinity.

This popular postcard view dates from the early years of this century and was taken from the Westgate Mill, probably from the sluice gates. The retaining wall and railings of The Causeway can be seen on the right of the picture. As with the above photograph, the building which dominates the view is the famous Abbott's Watermill. This lofty timber structure of six floors, plus observatory atop, was constructed in the early 1790s. It stood on the corner of Mill Lane and St Radigund's Street, opposite the Miller's Arms public house. In the 1880s both the Abbott's Mill and Westgate Mill were owned by the Canterbury artist Thomas Sidney Cooper.

The surviving square bastion from the city wall mentioned in the above caption can be seen here between the Abbott's Mill and Bell Harry Tower.

STOUR STREET

The old photograph featured here dates back to the early years of this century, when Stour Street contained many cottages and, therefore, many residents. It shows a group of houses that could be found on the east side of the street, between the junctions of Beer Cart Lane and Hawks Lane.

The picture is dominated by the two larger timber framed houses at Nos. 72 and 73 Stour Street. The central entrance is an access passage through to a group of humbler dwellings behind, known as Blue Coat Boy Cottages.

By the 1930s a number of changes to this scene had taken place. The white-painted cottages, seen to the left of the timber framed houses in the old picture, had been demolished and an open yard space created. The timber framed houses themselves had been smartened up, with the timbers picked out in black, and the plasterwork painted white. The building to the extreme right of the picture survived, and in the late 1930s was the premises of Miss Kate Fuller — confectioner.

The properties here sustained minor damage in one of the small hit and run raids on Canterbury in the autumn of 1940. They finally met their end in the major blitz of June 1942, when a number of buildings on the opposite side of Stour Street were also destroyed.

Wiltshiers builder's yard has now replaced the bombed properties, but traces of the cottages demolished before the war can still be found in the wall surrounding the yard. However, the builder's yard has been earmarked for residential redevelopment in the near future.

(Courtesy Derek Butler)

During the blitz, Stour Street was outside the main conflagration area, but suffered damage by high explosive bombs near the junction with Beer Cart Lane. This particular view was taken at that very junction in 1940 and looks up Stour Street. A significant building soon to come to grief was the medieval house in the foreground at No. 22 Stour Street. Since at least the turn of the century, this ancient timber framed structure had been part of the dry cleaning and dyeing works of E. Beasley and Son Ltd. Beasleys also operated from the adjoining properties at Nos. 23 and 24 Stour Street, both of which are visible in the picture.

The front half of the first storey of No. 22 was blown away in the blitz, but the remains of the building were patched up and lasted until the early 1960s. Then, Beasleys constructed a modern replacement building, which is now the Harvey Centre. (Their adjoining premises at No. 23 had already been rebuilt in the 1950s, and is also now part of the Harvey Centre.)

(Kent Messenger)

As mentioned on the opposite page, the pair of houses at Nos. 72 and 73 Stour Street later received a black and white colour scheme. They are seen here in this guise, pictured around 1940. The perimeter wall on the left of the picture consisted mainly of retained ground floor wall sections from the cottages demolished around ten years earlier. The old wall still survives today around Wiltshiers yard, and closer examination will reveal bricked up windows and doorways relating to buildings lost many years ago.

However, the timber framed cottages at Nos. 72 and 73 were victims of high explosive bombs. No. 72 and the smaller building to its right, the Fuller sweet shop, were completely destroyed in the Baedeker raid. The left hand cottage at No. 73 remained standing for a number of weeks after the raid, but its timber frame was so askew that it had to be demolished.

(Kent Messenger)

This third Kent Messenger view looks back down Stour Street with Beasleys' dye works in the distance. Many of these buildings are no longer standing, but the Luftwaffe are only partly to blame. In the foreground is No. 30 Stour Street, just before the turning into Stour Ville. This is followed by a group of three cottages, the nearest of which is three-storey, and may have been partly timber framed. The cottages were demolished in a mid 1960s slum clearance programme. Beyond these, and set back out of sight, is the Two Brewers public house at No. 26, which survives today as an office building.

Next is the premises of Douglas Charlton — wholesale confectioner (No. 25), followed by another ancient three-storey building at No. 24 Stour Street, then part of Beasleys' dye works. Nos. 24 and 25 were demolished around 1972 and eventually replaced by Stour Court.

(Kent Messenger)

THE ST MILDRED'S AREA

Between the world wars, the top end of Stour Street was dominated by the tannery buildings of J.J. Williamson and Sons on the river side of the street, very much as it does today. What has changed is the east side of Stour Street opposite St Mildred's Tannery.

The fascinating row of houses seen in the old photograph stood between the grounds of Maynard and Cotton's almshouses and the junction with Rosemary Lane. The picture dates from 1940, which would explain the anti-blast tape seen on the window panes of the house in the foreground. This attractive property is No. 62a Stour Street, occupied by one Mr Charles Turnbull.

Next to the brick house is a group of three-storey timber framed houses at Nos. 60 to 62, which are clearly of much greater age. Then, between these and the junction of Rosemary Lane in the distance, can be seen a row of brick built two-storey houses at Nos. 53 to 59 Stour Street. This row includes the grocers shop of Reginald Harris at No. 57.

All the houses featured in the old photograph survived the blitz of Canterbury, only to be demolished in a 'slum' clearance scheme in 1962. The site of the lost houses is now a surface car park. However, the lower walls of the front of the house at No. 62a Stour Street have survived, and form the perimeter wall to an extension of the almshouses gardens. This can be seen in the current picture, as can the surface car park further on.

The wall is certainly worth looking out for, as it contains the outline of a bricked up window complete with window sill, and the rendered door jambs of the former house still with a recess for the boot scraper.

(Kent Messenger)

Rosemary Lane is at right angles to the top of Stour Street, and runs up to Castle Street, which is itself parallel to Stour Street. During the years between the world wars two public houses could be found along the Lane's south side. The first of these, The Cardinal's Cap at No. 13, can still be seen today. In fact, it is the only building in Rosemary Lane to have survived the post-war demolition schemes. The other pub was the British Oak at Nos. 1 and 2 Rosemary Lane. It was closed for business as early as 1931 and is pictured here some ten years later, in a very dilapidated state. The pub remained empty and boarded up until the mid 1950s, when it was finally demolished. Even then, the ground floor walls survived as a perimeter wall to the site, until they too were finally removed in 1962.

(Kent Messenger)

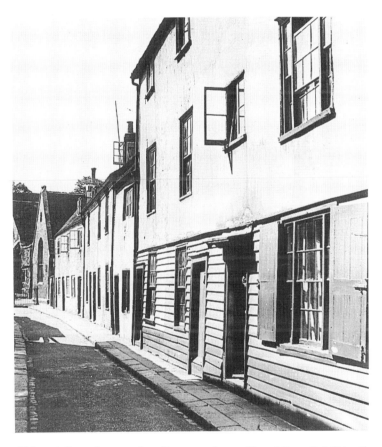

Church Lane St Mildred's takes its name from the ancient church with that dedication. Much Saxon work can be found in the south wall of the church, but what we can see in this picture is the east side, which is mostly medieval. For many years St Mildred's Church stood in the shadow of the city gas works. They were finally pulled down in 1968 and later replaced by the Rosemary Lane multi-storey car park.

(H.B. Collis)

Although Stour Street ends at Rosemary Lane, Church Lane St Mildred's continues along roughly the same trajectory and leads up to St Mildred's Church. The junction of all three roads can be seen in the top picture, as can some of the properties in Church Lane. The photograph here is a close-up view of those buildings along the west side of Church Lane St Mildred's. At the far end is the Church itself and, next to it, the church-like structure that was then Wincheap temporary council school. The two-storey cottages at Nos. 6 to 11 survived until 1962 when they were demolished as slums. The St John's Ambulance Brigade now have their headquarters building on this site. The four three-storey cottages in the foreground disappeared in the 1950s, and were replaced by a carpenter's workshop.

(Kent Messenger)

At the top end of Castle Street can be found the ruins of a substantial Norman Keep, from which the street obviously takes its name. This is an old post-card view, which dates from around the turn of the century. At this time the Castle Keep was in the hands of the gas company and used as a coal store. It surely must have been the oldest and most substantial coal bunker in England!

(H.B. Collis)

THE HIGH STREET

Until recent times little consideration was given to the antiquity or historical importance of a building in Canterbury considered to be either redundant, too old to renovate, or simply old-fashioned and ill-suited to an expanding modern business.

The old photograph, which dates from around 1885, features a group of such buildings in the High Street. The old buildings on the right of the picture, Nos. 48 and 49 High Street, would shortly be demolished and replaced by an impressive stone structure. This new building, completed in 1887, reflected the late Victorian tendency to mix several architectural styles together. For example, here we have a mixture of both Romanesque and Elizabethan features. At the turn of the century it was the premises of Fred Orchard — military and family bootmaker, and continued as such right up to the Second World War. Today it is the premises of the Abbey National Building Society.

Returning to the old picture, the old timber framed structure in the centre is the premises of Hobday and Ovenden — general ironmongers at No. 50 High Street. Just visible to the left is the old Canterbury Bank building on the corner of the High Street and St Margaret's Street. The Canterbury Bank was founded in 1788 by James Simmons, a one-time Mayor of Canterbury. Both the bank and ironmonger buildings were also subsequently demolished and replaced by a larger double fronted Canterbury bank that resembled a sort of Gothic-Elizabethan fortress.

The Canterbury bank merged with Lloyds Bank Ltd just after the First World War, and Lloyds are still there today.   (Fisk-Moore)

The story of Canterbury's old Guildhall was fully told in a double page feature in 'Canterbury Then and Now'. The main photograph in that book showed the Guildhall in the final years prior to its untimely demolition in 1950. The picture seen here was taken at a much earlier date, probably in the 1890s. The two pictures are worth comparing as the earlier view pre-dates the reconstruction of the side elevation along Guildhall Street. The work involved the removal of many of the windows and the addition of stucco and other decoration to match the neo-classical frontage to the High Street.

As stated in the aforementioned feature, much of the Victorian work on the Guildhall paid more attention to aesthetics than to the building's structural integrity. No doubt, this fact eventually contributed to the Guildhall's unfortunate demise.

(Fisk-Moore)

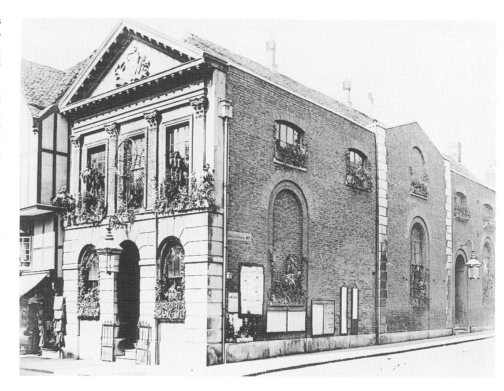

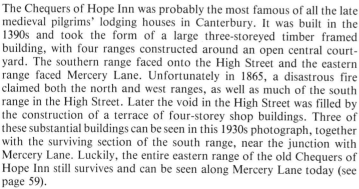

The Chequers of Hope Inn was probably the most famous of all the late medieval pilgrims' lodging houses in Canterbury. It was built in the 1390s and took the form of a large three-storeyed timber framed building, with four ranges constructed around an open central courtyard. The southern range faced onto the High Street and the eastern range faced Mercery Lane. Unfortunately in 1865, a disastrous fire claimed both the north and west ranges, as well as much of the south range in the High Street. Later the void in the High Street was filled by the construction of a terrace of four-storey shop buildings. Three of these substantial buildings can be seen in this 1930s photograph, together with the surviving section of the south range, near the junction with Mercery Lane. Luckily, the entire eastern range of the old Chequers of Hope Inn still survives and can be seen along Mercery Lane today (see page 59).

(Kent Messenger)

The essential character of Canterbury's High Street has been built up over many hundreds of years. This has been achieved by the gradual replacement of certain buildings from previous centuries by shops and houses in the current style of that time. Of course, other old buildings have been retained and adapted to new uses. The pictures on this page and the one opposite are representative of this process.

This particular view shows the new main Post Office nearing completion in 1908. Forty years earlier, the main Post Office had been set up on the same site, in an older building adapted to its new use. However, with the introduction and rapid expansion of the new telephone service, the old premises soon became inadequate, hence the building of the new Post Office.

(H.B. Collis)

Royal Fountain Hotel,
Canterbury. Tel. 185

ST MARGARET'S STREET

The Fountain Hotel in St Margaret's Street may have first come into
existence in the late Anglo-Saxon period. Early patrons were claimed to
be the wife of Earl Godwin in 1029 and Archbishop Lanfranc in 1070.
The name St Margaret's Street came into being when the church with
this dedication was established in the mid 12th century.

The old photograph shows the expansive Royal Fountain Hotel in the
1920s. It may have existed for nearly a thousand years, but this
particular building appears to be of 18th century origin! The prefix
'royal' was added in deference to Queen Victoria who, as their advertisement claimed, patronized the hotel on many occasions. The large
front entrance beneath the royal coat of arms led through to a courtyard
and extensive stables. However, by the time this picture was taken, the
stables had become garages for the patrons' motor cars, and offered
free of charge.

The Royal Fountain Hotel was completely destroyed in the Baedeker
raid of 1st June 1942, along with a number of other buildings on this
side of St Margaret's Street. Just visible to the right of the old
photograph is the Freemasons' Tavern. It adjoined the hotel and, as a
consequence, was seriously damaged by the blitz. However, what was
left of the tavern received a temporary roof and continued as a licensed
hostelry until 1965, when it was finally demolished.

For many years after the war the bombed site of the Royal Fountain
Hotel formed part of the Marlowe surface car park, as did the site of the
Freemasons' Tavern after its demise. Redevelopment finally came in the
early 1980s with the construction of the impressive Marlowe Arcade
complex.

(Fisk-Moore)

As mentioned opposite, the large hotel entrance from St Margaret's Street leads through to a courtyard and extensive stables. This photograph dates from around 1903 and looks out onto the courtyard area from a first floor hotel window. At this time the Royal Fountain Hotel stables were run by A.W. Anderson, the riding and job master. The services provided included carriages for weddings and funerals and horse drawn buses, as well as riding and driving taught by the proprietor himself.

The chimneys and roofs in the background belong to buildings along Rose Lane. Like the Royal Fountain Hotel, they too became victims of the blitz of Canterbury. Later, the entire site right up to Rose Lane became the Marlowe surface car park. Today the car park has given way to the Marlowe shopping arcade.

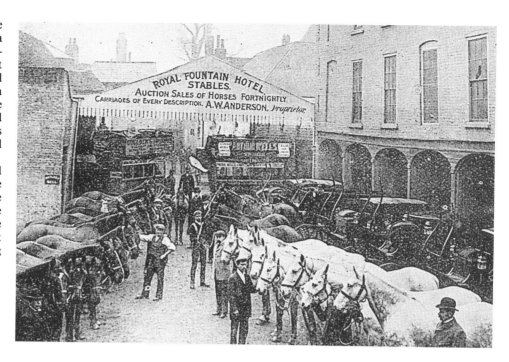

This photograph was taken in about 1940, and shows the part of the east side of St Margaret's Street nearest the junction with Watling Street. The St Margaret's Street buildings from left to right are: the premises of J.F. Duthoit, architect at No. 4, and next door at No. 3 is the St Margaret's Street Store run by Miss Nora Solley. Moving further along, the first of the medieval timber framed buildings appears to be empty but in the late 1930s was the premises of Fowler Brothers — dairymen. The further medieval building at the junction with Watling Street is the bakers' shop of Mrs E. Hogg at No. 1 St Margaret's Street. The grocery shop was destroyed in the blitz, but all the other buildings in this view survived. Today the site is occupied by an uninspiring concrete estate agents' buildings.

(Kent Messenger)

St Margaret's Street, a hundred years ago. This fascinating old photograph looks north along the street and captures many lost buildings along its east side. The imposing three-storey facade of the Royal Fountain Hotel stands out from the rest. However, what is even more fascinating are the lost timber framed buildings either side of the hotel. Most impressive of all is the double-jettied building with the three dormer windows, seen furthest from the camera. This building was still standing in the early years of this century, but was soon replaced by the three-storey double-fronted brick shop, now occupied by Waterstones.

Also of note is the three-storey timber framed building on this side of the Royal Fountain Hotel. This would be replaced in the mid 1920s by the new central picture theatre building that would later become the original Marlowe Theatre.

(Courtesy National Monuments Record)

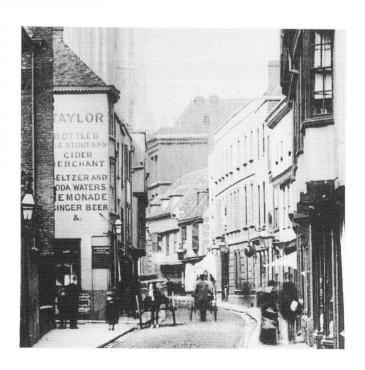

WATLING STREET

This fascinating Fisk-Moore photograph shows three early 17th century town houses in Watling Street.

The largest of the three and furthest from the camera is Sir John Mann's manor house, and dates from 1625. In the late 1930s it was the offices of Kingsford, Arrowsmith and Wightwick Solicitors at No. 16 Watling Street. This remarkable house was built of red brick with decorated stone courses. It has changed little since its construction, although the windows have been 'modernised', probably in the 18th century. Fortunately, this building survived the blitz of Canterbury and can be found in Watling Street today, still housing the same firm of solicitors.

The other two houses in the old picture, at Nos. 18 and 19 Watling Street, probably date from the same time as they were built in the Jacobean style, complete with Dutch gables; popular in the early 17th century. Prior to the Second World War No. 18 (Watling House) was the premises of the Kent Trade Protection Association Ltd. No. 19 (Watling Chambers) contained Hawkins and Roberts — analytical chemists, as well as the office of Mr Bowen, Clerk to the City Justices.

Unfortunately, these fine ivy-clad Jacobean houses were gutted in the fires of the June 1942 blitz. Immediately after the war a structural survey found that although the external walls were still standing, they were badly fire damaged and in urgent need of bracing and support. Therefore, it was decided that demolition was the only practical solution.

On a happier note, the modern office buildings, which have been built on the site of the lost houses, have been designed with the surviving 17th century house very much in mind. The result is a very successful blend of the old and new.

(Fisk-Moore, Courtesy Canterbury Museums)

This photograph dates from around 1900 and shows the Dane John Brewery, run by Ash and Company. These large premises stood on the corner of Watling Street and Marlowe Avenue, and extended along the entire east side of the latter thoroughfare. In this building Ash's brewed 'Canterbury Ales', stout and porter (the latter being a dark brown malt liquor).

The brewery was not a victim of the blitz, but was demolished in the 1930s. The site subsequently became a surface car park, as it still is some sixty years later. Remnants of the brewery can still be found today; the low perimeter wall along Marlowe Avenue once formed part of the actual brewery building wall. However, within the next ten years the car park is likely to be re-developed as part of the overall Whitefriars development scheme.

This tele-photo shot was taken from the Dane John in 1937 and looks towards the Cathedral across the buildings of Watling Street and Rose Lane. The empty site just beyond the lopped trees was, until rcently, occupied by Ash's Brewery as seen in the top photograph, but from the opposite direction. The houses in Watling Street on either side of the junction with Rose Lane can clearly be seen in this view. They were demolished in the early 1960s, but many of the buildings further along Rose Lane were victims of the bombing. The largest and most impressive of these was the Church of St Mary Bredin, which clearly stands out in this panoramic view. St Mary Bredin's Church is considered in more detail on pages 20 and 21.

(Fisk-Moore)

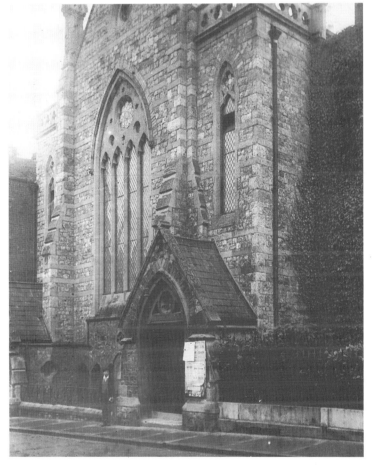

Watling Street Church was built in 1863 for an offshoot of the congregational faith known as the Countess of Huntingdon's Connexion. The church building was symmetrical in design with an entrance porch on either side of the large Gothic style window, although only one of these is visible in the old photograph. The church was a victim of the Canterbury blitz, although not on the night of the main Baedeker raid of 1st June 1942. It succumbed during one of the minor raids in the following week, when enemy aircraft attempted to complete their prime objective of destroying the Cathedral; a job thankfully never successfully carried out. In the late 1940s a temporary prefabricated church appeared on the site, followed by a permanent replacement around ten years later.

ROSE LANE

Pre-war Rose Lane was dominated by the neo-Gothic church of St Mary Bredin. This beautiful building was most noteworthy for its octagonal tower and spire, which can clearly be seen in the old photograph, taken by W. Fisk-Moore in the 1930s.

St Mary Bredin's was built in 1868, replacing a smaller 13th century church on the same site. The larger Victorian church also took up much of the old graveyard, so a new burial ground was brought into use, in nearby Gravel Walk.

On the left of the picture can be seen the gates leading into the forecourt of Crows Ltd, a wholesale motor car accessories concern. In the late 1930s a large corrugated garage building would be constructed within the forecourt, roughly where the tree stands in the old picture.

Just visible on the right of Rose Lane is part of the premises of W.S. Williams & Son — Coachbuilders.

Regrettably, St Mary Bredin Church and much of Rose Lane was destroyed by fire, caused by thousands of incendiary bombs dropped on Canterbury in the small hours of 1st June 1942. The badly fire-damaged octagonal tower and surviving church walls were dismantled in the months that followed the blitz.

The last visible traces of the church finally disappeared in 1952 during road widening operations along Rose Lane. However, the remote burial ground could still be found along Gravel Walk well into the 1960s.

Today the site of St Mary Bredin's Church is partly occupied by the Marlowe shopping arcade, and partly by a much widened Rose Lane.

(Fisk-Moore)

Rose Lane was at its narrowest along the section between Gravel Walk and Canterbury's main street. Along this stretch on the west side could be found a few cottages, some small warehouses, a public house, the Fountain Tap, and several rear entrance passageways. One led to the rear courtyard and stables of the Royal Fountain Hotel (see pages 16 and 17).

Nearer the main street end could be found the rear courtyard access for the Rose Hotel, and then finally the side of the hotel itself. This fascinating photograph clearly shows that the side of the Rose Hotel in Rose Lane was made up from a number of old buildings. The double-jettied timber framed building is of particular interest. Just visible in the background is the Corn Exchange and Longmarket building in the main street.

(Rob Williams)

The junction of Rose Lane with Canterbury's main street marks the point where St George's Street ends and The Parade begins. On the Parade Corner stood the Rose Hotel, the subject of this photograph. The hotel was established in 1660, the same year as the restoration of the monarchy. In fact Charles II visited pro-royalist Canterbury on his way back to London to take up the throne, but it is not known if he stayed at the Rose Hotel! The main section of the hotel fronting The Parade was clearly rebuilt in the late 18th century, although part of the Rose Lane elevation was much older, as the top picture illustrates.

Just before the blitz, the Rose Hotel closed and was being offered for let when the Fisk-Moore studio photographed it. The Rose Hotel was gutted in the Baedeker raid, as was most of Rose Lane along the section nearest the main street.

(Fisk-Moore, Courtesy Canterbury Museums)

The Rose Lane that existed before the Second World War was very different from the wide thoroughfare we know today. In fact the only similarity is that the lane had two distinct sections, as it does now, on either side of the junction with Gravel Walk. This picture shows the section from Watling Street to Gravel Walk, and was taken from further back than the view opposite. St Mary Bredin Church stands opposite the aforementioned Gravel Walk junction.

The warehouses seen here on either side of the lane were damaged in the minor raids of June 1942, and again during the daylight attack of 31st October 1942. Part of the premises of Williams Coachbuilders survived the onslaught, and lasted until as recently as 1965. Today there is nothing in Rose Lane that could be found in the years before the blitz of Canterbury.

(Courtesy Derek Butler)

(Above) The Causeway and St Stephen's Road area, with the West Station coalyard at the top of the picture. The, then, recently constructed East Kent bus garage is in the centre. Also note the Westgate Mill at the junction of The Causeway with St Stephen's Road and the houses of St Stephen's Field situated between the mill and goods yard.

(Kentish Gazette)

(Below) Cityscape looking north-east. The lines of buildings along Burgate Street and The Parade/St George's Street can just be made out. The lush vegetation of the former monastic houses of Greyfriars (bottom right) and Blackfriars (bottom left) can be discerned, as can the many trees then to be found in the Cathedral precincts.

(Kentish Gazette)

(Above) A general view of the south-west part of Canterbury including the suburb of Wincheap, the East Railway Station, the Dane John and St Mildred's area. Note the covered roof of the East Station, removed in the 1950s. Also of interest is the Canterbury Waverley Football Club ground on the left of the picture, now occupied by Telephone House.
(Kentish Gazette)

(Below) A closer view than the one above of the gas works at the top of Castle Street and the Wincheap Green area. Note, the old Norman Keep is full of coal for the gas works! It was the ring road in the early 1960s, and not the blitz, that caused the destruction of many buildings in this view. Other losses include St Andrew's Church (bottom) and the houses of Rosemary Lane.

(Kentish Gazette)

ST GEORGE'S STREET — WEST END

Canterbury's main street bears a number of different names on its half mile journey from the Westgate to St George's Gate. The old photograph was taken from the St George's Street section and looks down The Parade and then along the High Street section beyond.

The south side of St George's Street can just be seen on the left. On this side, the St George's Street numbering went down as far as Rose Lane and the Baker's Temperance Hotel at Nos. 30 and 31. On the more visible north side, the numbering extended further, and down to the junction with Butchery Lane. On the extreme right of the picture the National Provincial Bank at No.25 St George's Street can just be seen. Next is the imposing neo-classical facade of the Canterbury Corn and Hop Exchange building. Within its walls were also the Longmarket and J.H.G. Hamilton wine merchants.

Beyond the Corn Exchange is Robert Crofts chemist and Walter Hart

chiropodist at No. 27. This is followed by the premises of Taylor Bros. Corn and Seed Merchants (No. 28) and, finally, on the corner with Butchery Lane at No. 29 St George's Street is the tailors, Burton Montague Ltd. Beyond Butchery Lane the many shops of The Parade can be seen.

St George's Street caught the full brunt of the blitz of Canterbury, and was mostly destroyed by fire from the thousands of incendiary bombs dropped on this part of Canterbury. Butchery Lane became a fire break, with the result that all the buildings on the St George's Street side of the junction were destroyed, whilst those on The Parade side survived.

At the time of writing, the large 'Longmarket' site is being re-developed for the third time since the blitz.

(Fisk-Moore)

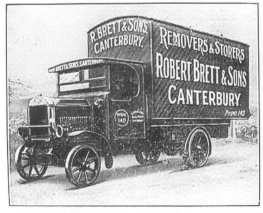

ONE OF THE FLEET OF OUR LONG-DISTANCE REMOVAL VANS

This Fisk-Moore picture has appeared many times in print before, but still deserves a place on this page. It shows the lovely neo-classical frontage of the Canterbury Corn and Hop Exchange building, which also encompassed the Longmarket on the ground floor. The photograph was taken in 1940 and shows the war savings indicator with its motto 'No Limit to Lending'. The building was seriously damaged in the main blitz and, although the main frontage survived, it was nevertheless demolished within days of the raid. However, small sections of the Corn Exchange and Longmarket building were retained and survived well into the 1950s (see 'Canterbury Then and Now', pages 8, 9, 16 and 17).

(Fisk-Moore, Courtesy Canterbury Museums)

As mentioned opposite, the last building on the southside of St George's Street, on the corner with Rose Lane, was the Baker's Temperance Hotel. This large double-fronted building is pictured here and can also be seen in the large view opposite, towards the left. However, by the late 1930s the Baker's Temperance Hotel had been relocated to Ivy Lane (now the Chaucer Hotel), and their former premises was now called Parade Chambers. This encompassed several businesses including the Eagle Star Insurance Company and the Pilgrim's Teahouse run by Mrs M. White.

There was nothing left of this impressive building following the raid of 1st June 1942. The site remained empty for another ten years and was then used to widen Rose Lane.

(Courtesy Derek Butler)

This photograph was taken at about the turn of the century and shows the three-storey Georgian building next to the Corn Exchange in St George's Street. At this time it was the premises of Hilton C. Price: Wine, Spirit and Cigar Merchant. By the 1920s the ground floor had been taken over by the National Provincial Bank, and the plain ground-floor frontage had been re-faced with ornate brickwork. (Some of this work is just visible to the right of the picture opposite.)

Above the bank could be found the St George's Private Hotel, with Miss Wilson as proprietress. Later, the hotel gave way to a firm of auctioneers and estate agents.

This building was also a blitz victim. Very soon after its destruction, a temporary bank building appeared on the site, followed by a permanent replacement in 1956.

HILTON C. PRICE,
Wine, Spirit & Cigar Merchant,
26 St. George's Street,
CANTERBURY.

THE SIMON LANGTON SCHOOLS

The old photograph featured here dates from the 1930s and shows a section of the original 1881 development of the Simon Langton schools at Whitefriars.

The name Whitefriars comes from the order of friars which had existed on the site from 1325 until the Reformation. These Augustinian, or Austin, friars wore white habits, thus distinguishing themselves from the Dominican Blackfriars and the Franciscan Greyfriars.

The 1930's picture includes part of the boys' school on the left of the range, and a portion of the girls' school at the other end. The middle two-storey section is the two private residences of the boys' headmaster, Mr Leonard Myers, and the girls' headmistress, Miss Nora Campling.

The boys and girls were strictly segregated with their own dedicated buildings and areas of playground. The only time the girls strayed onto the boys' territory was to use their Gymnasium in the 'new' 1914 extension block along the St George's Lane edge of the Whitefriars site.

In the school grounds there were reminders of the Whitefriars' historical past, as the old perimeter wall along Rose Lane and Gravel Walk contained medieval material. More significant was a surviving length of wall that was once part of the west wall of the friary church. It was situated near to the girls' entrance from St George's Street, and can just be seen on the extreme right of the old picture.

The wartime bomb damage sustained by the Simon Langton School buildings was so severe that the girls were forced to move elsewhere. The boys remained at Whitefriars in the remains of both schools and, with the help of some additional pre-fabricated buildings, carried on until 1959.

(Kentish Gazette)

As mentioned on the opposite page, the boys and girls were strictly segregated, despite their respective buildings being adjoined and in the same grounds. However, this rule was broken in July of 1931 when the schools reached their jubilee; being fifty years since they had opened. The anniversary was celebrated by a rare joint venture, involving both boys and girls. This took the form of a costumed pageant and was performed on the tennis courts in the girls' section of the school grounds. The Fisk-Moore photograph shows a number of the participants assembled for the camera. Behind the costumed children can be seen a section of the old Whitefriars perimeter wall and, beyond this, the rear of a number of buildings along the south side of St George's Street.

(Fisk-Moore)

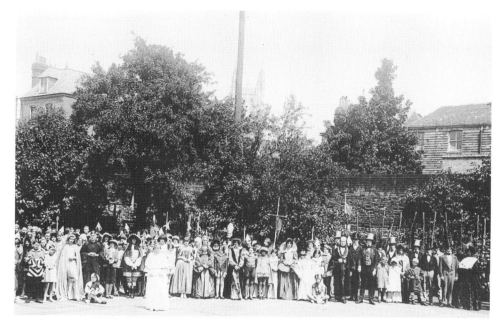

The entrance to the girls' part of the Simon Langton School was from St George's Street (see page 29). Having passed through the street gateway and along the passage, a second gate would have been reached. From here the girls could approach their part of the school building now in front of them, as the photograph illustrates. The small gateway to the left in the picture leads to the residences of the head-mistress, then onto the headmaster's house and the boys' part of the school grounds. The garden area seen on the right was known as 'The Orchard', and was an ideal place to rest and relax in between exams.

In the blitz of Canterbury about ninety per cent of the girls' school was lost. However, a small section of the building to the right of the picture survived, and was used by the boys' school until 1959.

When the Second World War was declared, Canterbury became a reception town for evacuated children from London and the Medway towns. Simon Langton Boys' School shared their buildings with Erith County School, and the girls shared with St Joseph's Convent, Abbey Wood. However, by May 1940, the threat of invasion had greatly increased, and all children who had been evacuated to Canterbury were re-evacuated to South Wales.

Then, in September of the same year, Canterbury children themselves were evacuated, again mainly to South Wales. This picture shows many school children of varying ages awaiting embarkation at Canterbury East Station. In the same month, half the Simon Langton Girls' School was evacuated to Reading, then in October, half the Boys' School went to Wantage in Berkshire.

However, as 1941 progressed and no bombs fell on Canterbury in that year, most evacuated children drifted back to the city.

(Rob Williams)

ST GEORGE'S STREET — MIDDLE SECTION

Before the Second World War, St George's Street was an attractive thoroughfare, with an assortment of buildings of differing ages and styles on both sides. It was the sort of street scene that can be found in St Peter's Street or the High Street today, both of which were largely unaffected by the blitz of Canterbury.

This view of St George's Street, looking east, was taken in the early years of this century when there was little or no motor traffic. However, by the 1930s traffic was very much in evidence. Hold-ups were not uncommon, especially if there was a funeral at St George's Church, when a policeman was required to direct the traffic.

St George's Street was wiped out in one fell swoop in the small hours of 1st June 1942. In the days that followed, any burnt out shells of brick buildings still standing were quickly demolished. Only the gutted ruins of St George's Church were left standing. Eventually, just the tower was kept and restored, despite moves from certain quarters to have it removed.

From 1944 onwards the Canterbury excavation committee carried out a number of archaeological digs amongst the ruined cellars on both sides of St George's Street. The most impressive find in this section was a Roman bath house, situated where Woolworths and W.H. Smith stand today. A large Roman house was also discovered under the street in front of St George's Church.

St George's Street was re-developed, mostly in the years 1951 to 1956, and widened in 1952.

(Courtesy Derek Butler)

The shops in this view can also be seen in the picture on page 28 to the left. This close up photograph is another from the Fisk-Moore pictorial record of 1941, and captures some interesting buildings on the north side of St George's Street. The shop on the far left is the premises of Austens — circulating library and stationers. Next door, the building with the tiled front elevation and double jetty is Thomas Goodman, the cutler, at No. 16 St George's Street. The white bow-fronted shop adorned with war savings posters is Wards the confectioners. Following the main raid of June 1942 nothing save rubble-filled cellars could be found on the north side of the street, between Barclays Bank and the ruins of St George's Church.

(Fisk-Moore, Courtesy Canterbury Museums)

The three photographs on this page show close-up views of buildings that could once be found on either side of St George's Street. Barclays Bank is not visible in the large view opposite as it was situated further down towards the Corn Exchange on the street's north side. This Fisk-Moore picture dates from 1941 and shows the aforementioned bank at No. 23 St George's Street. To the right is the newly built premises of the Co-operative Insurance Society Ltd, with Dolcis Shoe Shop on the ground floor.

The new shop was completely destroyed in the blitz, and the bank premises were severely damaged. However, the ground floor section of Barclays was retained until the early 1950s when it gave way to today's Barclays Bank, constructed on the same site.

(Fisk-Moore, Courtesy Canterbury Museums)

On the south side of St George's Street, and virtually opposite the shops in the above picture, could be found the entrance gateway to the Simon Langton Girls School. (The boys entered from Gravel Walk, adjacent to their Science block.) The gateway was built in a perpendicular Gothic style, and was possibly a Victorian reconstruction using demolition material recovered from the old Whitefriars. In any event, this attractive structure was restored in the 1930s, under the auspices of Alderman Charles Lefevre.

The gateway was destroyed in the blitz, but the passageway beyond continued to be used as access to the school grounds. Consequently, when the new terrace of shops was constructed here in 1952, a passageway was included. Today this allows access to the Whitefriars Shopping Centre.

(Fisk-Moore, Courtesy Canterbury Museums)

ST GEORGE'S CHURCH

The origin of St George's Church can now be dated with more certainty, following the recent archaeological investigation of the clock tower site. It was probably first built in the last twenty-five years of the 11th century, making its construction concurrent with that of Lanfranc's Cathedral. The lower part of the tower is substantially 12th century, and an original round-topped Romanesque doorway survives on its west side. The church was subsequently rebuilt and extended on a number of occasions over the next three centuries.

This fine old postcard view of St George's Church was taken between the world wars. The perpendicular style windows along the south wall of the nave replaced the originals in the 15th century. Another minor alteration was the removal of a staircase turret that adjoined the tower on its south side.

Then, in 1872, a major extension of the church to the north and east was started. This was prompted by the closure of St Mary Magdalene six years earlier, and its subsequent demolition. (The two parishes had amalgamated many years before.) The population of both parishes had also greatly increased. Columns and arches from the demolished St Mary Magdalene Church were recovered and re-used in the new expanded St George's.

St George's Church was destroyed by fire in the blitz of Canterbury, and survived in ruin until late 1952, when all but the tower was demolished. The tower itself was extensively restored in the following two years.

In 1955 an arcade of austere modern shops was constructed around the clock tower. These were demolished in 1991, just prior to the aforementioned archaeological dig. The 'current' view on this page was taken just days before the demolition.

Construction of a new arcade of shops was about to begin at the time of writing.

This is one of only a few known pictures of the ancient font at St George's Church. It was thought to date from the 13th century, and reflects the Early English Gothic style of the time. The font was octagonal, but had only seven outer columns; the eighth was missing to allow the officiating priest closer access. There was also a large bell-shaped lid, but this is not visible in the photograph.

The font was situated at the west end of the central aisle (the north aisle before the Victorian extension) and was therefore just north of the clock tower. A number of famous people were baptised here, amongst them playwright Christopher Marlowe in 1564. The font was destroyed along with the majority of the church in the infamous Baedeker raid. The archaeological dig of 1991 failed to find any trace of it.

(H.B. Collis)

Also at the west end of the church, but in the 'new' northern aisle, could be found the Warriors Corner. On the wall here was a bronze memorial which read: 'To the glory of God and in undying memory of the officers and men who gave their lives for King and Country in the naval action at Zeebrugge, Saint George's Day 1918. This tablet is erected by their admiral, some of their comrades and the Kent branch of the Royal Society of Saint George'.

There was also a flag on the wall which had been used in making the signal 'Saint George for England', on the eve of the aforementioned naval action.

However, what dominated Warriors Corner was an altar or shrine made of wood salvaged from HMS *Vindictive*, and this can be seen in the accompanying photograph.

(Courtesy Derek Butler)

This fascinating view of the east end of St George's Church comes from an old postcard, originally taken at Eastertime in 1923. For all its Gothic splendour, much of what you can see here belongs to the Victorian enlargement of the church in 1872. The central aisle extends into the new chancel, where the altar is situated. The columns and arches on the right are part of the arcade erected at the same time as the Victorian extension. It replaced a row of iron columns, which had themselves replaced the original medieval columns between the two aisles of the earlier church. The first arch in the arcade between the central aisle and the 'new' north aisle is just visible on the left. Much of this consisted of materials recovered from the demolished Church of St Mary Magdalene in Burgate Street.

(Courtesy Derek Butler)

ST GEORGE'S LANE

This amazing cityscape was captured in 1937 by Joyce Cozens from her third floor bedroom window, using a box brownie camera. At this time she lived at No. 13 St George's Terrace which was one of the large three-storey houses built along the top of the city wall. What the young photographer could not have realised was that nearly every building in this view would perish in the awful Baedeker raid, just five years later.

From the back of the houses along St George's Terrace one looked down onto St George's Lane. The roofs and chimneys of the cottages along the east side of the lane can be seen in the immediate foreground. Running between the cottages and the rear of the St George's Terrace houses was Sheepshank Alley, a tiny foot passage.

The buildings along the west side of St George's Lane were more substantial. On the left, with its hipped roof end towards the camera, is the large house at No. 13 St George's Lane. Further to the right at No. 14 was the large premises of J.A. Jennings Ltd, printer. This adjoined the Bridge Court studio, wherein could be found Miss Ianthe Bridge, teacher of the pianoforte, and Miss Peggy Court, teacher of dancing.

In the middle distance can be seen the various roofs of the buildings along St George's Street, and the tower and spire of St George's Church to the right. The Cathedral, of course, dominates the picture from the background. Apart from St George's clock tower, it is the only building in the old picture still standing today, although Riceman's massive modern building prevents it from being seen from the same position along the city wall.

(Joyce Cozens)

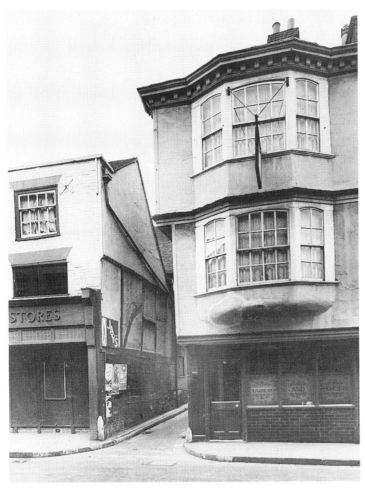

Considering today's wide thoroughfare, it is hard to believe that this is a picture of St George's Lane at its junction with St George's Street. The building on the left is of particular interest. It is No. 57 St George's Street, reputed to be the birthplace of Christopher Marlowe. At the time this photograph was taken, in 1941, Jays Furnishing House occupied the building, as well as the adjoining property at No. 58. The larger building on the right of St George's Lane is the Coach and Horses public house at No. 56 St George's Street. Both properties were destroyed in the blitz of Canterbury. The pub was re-built further up a much widened St George's Lane in the early 1960s. It has recently been re-named the Fools and Horses, but is ultimately destined to be demolished under the Whitefriars redevelopment scheme.

(Fisk-Moore, Courtesy Canterbury Museums)

Further along the south side of St George's Street, and virtually opposite St George's Church tower, could be found the premises of William Pollard, jeweller and watchmaker. This picture comes from the 1924 official guide to Canterbury and clearly shows the handsome lines of this old timber framed building. It dated from the 15th century and was probably one of the oldest shops in St George's Street. During alterations carried out in the early 1920s the then existing tiled covering was removed from the front elevation to reveal the oak timbers for the first time in many years. The larger brick building to the right is the tobacconist of Howard K. Fullager; a shop with the curious number of 52½ St George's Street! Alas, both shops were further victims of the Canterbury bombing.

This is another old cityscape photograph from the box brownie camera of Joyce Cozens. In 1938 the Cozens family moved from No. 13 St George's Terrace to a smaller house at No. 1. The rear of their new property overlooked another stretch of St George's Lane, as well as the backs of the buildings on either side of the lane's junction with St George's Street. On the far right is the white rear gable of No. 57, and next to it, the tiled three-storey rear elevation of the Coach and Horses.

To the left of the pub is London Outfitters Ltd (No. 55), followed by F.W. Woolworth & Co. Ltd (No. 54) and, finally, the rear of Pollards jewellers at No. 53.

The tower and spire of St George's Church stands behind the miscellany of old roofs, proudly flying the flag of England and St George.

(Joyce Cozens)

ST GEORGE'S GATE

St George's Gate was the short section of the main street through Canterbury between the crossroads with Upper and Lower Bridge Street and the junction of St George's Terrace and Burgate Lane. It was so named as it was on the site of the old St George's city gate that had been demolished in 1801.

The old photograph is a popular postcard view of St George's Gate taken from the aforementioned crossroads, looking towards St George's Street. The shops of St George's Gate can be seen in the foreground on the right. In the immediate foreground is the tiled front elevation of No. 1 St George's Gate; the premises of Pettit and Sons, tobacconists. At No. 2 is the piano shop of Godfrey & Co. Ltd. Later in the 1930s this shop had become F.W. Finnis, the baker. No. 3, partially obscured by the lamp post, is A.T. Bates, gunsmith, who also traded in cycles and motor vehicles. Nos. 4 and 5 St George's Gate are the photographic studio of B. & W. Fisk-Moore. In the 1930s the Fisk-Moore studio moved to No. 7 St George's Place. No. 4 St George's Gate then became the Fisk-Moore retail shop, and No. 5 was taken over by King and Son — hosiers.

On the night of 1st June 1942 St George's Gate caught the full fury of the blitz of Canterbury, and Nos. 2 to 5 were destroyed, along with many other buildings in the St George's area.

Pettits tobacconist at No. 1 survived right until 1969, when it was demolished to make way for St George's roundabout.

Although Bates gun shop at No. 3 had been destroyed, the firm continued to trade from a wooden hut within the ruined walls of their old premises. This, too, finally disappeared in 1969, as did the street name of St George's Gate.

(Courtesy Derek Butler)

This view of the top end of St George's Street is probably the Fisk-Moore Studio's most well known photograph of pre-war Canterbury. St George's Gate is situated just beind the photographer. The picture includes many buildings that are shown in detail on other pages in this volume. St George's Parish Church can clearly be seen on the north side of St George's Street (see also pages 30 and 31). Many of the shops on the street's south side are also visible here. Nearest the camera are Jays Furnishing Stores and the Coach and Horses public house on either side of the junction with St George's Lane. Further along on the same side is William Pollard the jeweller (page 33). In this view the jeweller's shop still carries the tiles on the front elevation, obscuring the medieval timbers beneath.

(Fisk-Moore)

This wonderful ivy clad building could once be found on the corner of St George's Terrace and St George's Street. It is one of a group of adjoining structures known as the Sun Buildings. This particular building is the Sun Insurance Office. The other associated premises were situated to its left, and partially up the slope of St George's Terrace. They included the Sun Life Assurance Society offices and solicitor and chartered accountant premises.

The photograph dates from the late 1930s and makes an interesting comparison with the earlier view on the opposite page, which also includes this building. It is clear that in the intervening years, a new corner doorway was cut in and one of the windows bricked over. All of the Sun Buildings were destroyed in the blitz. In 1957 a new Sun Building was constructed on the same site, but has since passed into other hands.

(Courtesy R.E. Cranfield)

This photograph of St George's Gate was taken in the opposite direction to all the other views on this page and the one on page 34. Probably dating from the late 1930s, it shows the crossroads of St George's Gate and St George's Place with Upper and Lower Bridge Street. The view includes a number of buildings that survived the bombing, but only one that can be seen today. Of the blitz victims, the row of shops on the left succumbed in the Baedeker raid of June 1942. These included the Fisk-Moore retail shop and A.T. Bates' gunsmith and cycle shop.

Then, as a result of the October 1942 daylight raid, a large section of the Regal Cinema nearest the camera and the two adjacent shops were completely destroyed. These can be seen beyond the crossroads on the right.

The remaining buildings were demolished in 1969 (see opposite). The only survivor today is the Regal Cinema which was repaired and is now the Cannon.

(Fisk-Moore)

ST GEORGE'S TERRACE

When walking today along the city wall above the bus station it is hard to believe that there was once a succession of two- and three-storey houses built along its entire length. A number of these can be seen in the old photograph, taken by the Kent Messenger around 1940. In the foreground are the two-storey buildings at Nos. 2 to 5 St George's Terrace. They were situated on the gradual slope down from the city wall, which led onto St George's Street, behind the camera.

The first of the three-storey buildings is the Spirella corset house at No. 6, run by Mrs Sims, a corsetiere. Then there was a continual succession of elegant Georgian houses right up to No. 25 St George's Terrace. Beyond these houses Gravel Walk sloped away from the city wall to the right, down to ground level. St George's Terrace continued along the city wall for a further fifty yards or so, before sloping down to Watling Street. As today, one could also continue along the city wall and over the Riding Gate.

Between the Gravel Walk slope and Watling Street stood a larger house at No. 26 St George's Terrace. It was the private residence of Charles Dunkin, named Terrace House. Mr Dunkin had a veterinary practice along nearby St George's Lane and also owned stables attached to his house on St George's Terrace.

The terrace was virtually wiped out in the Baedeker raid of 1st June 1942. The burnt out shells of the once grand town houses must have been a sad sight indeed.

Today St George's Terrace has no buildings of its own, and even its name is not often used anymore.

(Kent Messenger)

36

This fascinating view of the old cattle market, with St George's Terrace behind, dates from about 1903. It becomes immediately apparent that the residents of the Terrace had the dubious honour of overlooking the regularly held cattle market, situated between the city wall and Upper Bridge Street. A number of pre-war postcard views give a very romantic impression of the market with its jolly drovers, well groomed livestock and busy market folk. This was certainly very much part of it, but there was another side to consider. Residents of St George's Terrace could have told you how the overwhelming smell made it impossible to open any windows in the summer, or how disturbing it could be to watch the poor animals being hit by the drovers.

The wonderful photograph here looks right along the city wall and includes nearly every building that existed along St George's Terrace. It dates from 1940 and comes from the archives of the Kent Messenger. No. 13 St George's Terrace, the first residence of the Cozens family (see page 32) is the three-storey brick house to the left of the stuccoed houses. No. 13 jutted further forward as it fronted directly onto St George's Terrace. Most other properties had their own small area at the front with railings, and steps leading up to the front door.

In the foreground the disassembled pens of the cattle market lean against the city wall. The original medieval city wall bastions had been removed many years before.

After the blitz, and the destruction of all the houses along St George's Terrace, the city wall was restored to something like its late medieval appearance.

(Kent Messenger)

The final picture features the aforementioned stuccoed three-storey houses at Nos. 6 to 12 St George's Terrace. As mentioned opposite, No. 6, on the far right of this view, was the corsetiere business of Mrs C. Sims. Nos. 7 to 11 were exclusively private residences and, in the 1937 Street Directory, were occupied by: Mr Charles Morris (No. 7), Mr Thomas Harrison (No. 8), Mrs Deer (No. 10) and Mr Edward Hearn (No .11). No. 9 was temporarily unoccupied at this time. No. 12 St George's Terrace was the premises of Smith and Cross, servants registry office, as well as the residence of Mr Percy Uden. St George's Terrace suffered terribly on the night of the Baedeker raid, 1st June 1942. No. 6 received a direct hit from a high explosive bomb, whilst Nos. 7 to 12 were all gutted by incendiary bomb fires.
(Fisk-Moore, Courtesy Canterbury Museums)

UPPER BRIDGE STREET

The attractive row of cottages in the old photograph could once be found along Upper Bridge Street in front of the city wall. In 1830 a walled city pound was established between Upper Bridge Street and the city wall, under the auspices of the city chamberlain, Alderman Warren. The cottages at Nos. 18 to 24 Upper Bridge Street were probably built at around the same time. The city's defensive moat had already been filled in along this stretch and much of the medieval city wall with its bastions had been demolished. The city wall had then been rebuilt, substantially of red brick.

The featured cottages were situated between the Riding Gate on the left and the city pound to the right, where the regular cattle markets were held. Unfortunately, they fell victim to the blitz of Canterbury, although the Riding Gate Inn, just visible to the left of the picture, survived until 1955. In January of that year the pub was demolished to make way for the Riding Gate roundabout.

Part of the city pound perimeter wall can just be seen to the right of the old photograph. This was demolished in September 1955, shortly after the cattle market had been transferred to a new purpose-built site at St Stephen's. The old city pound, together with the site of the blitzed cottages, continued in use as a surface car park.

Construction of a replica of the medieval city wall in flint was begun in 1958. This work included the reconstruction of two of the three bastions, which had at one time existed between the Riding Gate and St George's Gate.

The last traces of the city pound and former cattle market disappeared in 1969, when Upper Bridge Street was dualled as part of the second stage of the ring road construction.

(Fisk-Moore, Courtesy Canterbury Museums)

The Riding Gate was originally a Roman city gate through which Watling Street passed. It is clear from contemporary drawings that traces of the actual Roman gate survived until about 1782, when Riding Gate was completely demolished. A red bricked arch replaced the former gate in 1791, at about the same time as the Dane John public gardens were first created. That particular version of the Riding Gate is pictured here, just before its own removal, in the early 1880s. The photographer is standing at Riding Gate crossroads, with Upper Bridge Street to his right, and Rhodaus Town and the old moat to his left.

The brick archway was replaced by an iron bridge in 1883. This Victorian Riding Gate lasted until 1970, when today's bland concrete version was constructed.

(Kentish Gazette)

A fascinating view of the cattle market as it appeared in 1941. It was taken from St George's Terrace and is therefore a reverse view from those which appear on page 37. The buildings in Upper Bridge Street can just be seen behind the lush summer foliage of the trees along the edge of the cattle market. St George's crossroads is on the far left, and the junction with Dover Street just out of sight on the right. Bomb damage along this stretch of Upper Bridge Street was severe, although the buildings nearest the crossroads survived.

Most of the trees and railings in this view were removed in 1956. The remainder went in 1969 when the site of the old cattle market finally disappeared to make way for the ring road.

(Rob Williams)

This 1941 photograph is another from the extensive building record, undertaken thankfully before the blitz of Canterbury. These single-storey cottages could be found opposite the cattle market and were numbered 12 to 17 Upper Bridge Street. In 1937 these humble dwellings were all occupied by ladies, namely Mrs Wilson, Miss Elvey, Mrs Cole, Miss Keene, Mrs Neil and Mrs Uden respectively. The large three-storey building to the left was then the offices of Drapers and General Insurance Co. Ltd and the Provincial Insurance Co. Ltd. All of the buildings seen here survived the blitz intact. The tiny cottages were demolished in 1963 to make way for Lombard House, a modern office block. The three-storey building at No. 11 Upper Bridge Street survives today.

(Fisk-Moore, Courtesy Canterbury Museums)

THE DANE JOHN

This idyllic scene, captured by the Fisk-Moore studio in the 1940s,
shows the old moat that was once part of the Dane John Gardens. It
could be found between Worthgate Place and the Riding Gate, running
round the outside of the city wall. The medieval city wall can be seen
between the many trees.

The Romans were the first to build a defensive wall and ditch around
Canterbury. When the Normans took over in the 11th century, they
re-used the Roman city wall and gates, which had survived reasonably
well. Later, in medieval times, the wall was substantially rebuilt and
many square and 'D' shaped bastions were constructed around the
entire circumference. The city gates were also rebuilt, but over a much
longer period of time.

A defensive ditch or moat existed round the outside of the city wall,
except by the Westgate where the River Stour offered adequate protection.

From the 1700s onwards significant lengths of the now redundant city
wall were dismantled for building material, and much of the defensive
moat was filled in and developed. Only one section of the old moat
lasted into this century, which is that seen in the old photograph. Its
survival was due to it being absorbed into the Dane John, created by
Alderman James Simmons in the 1790s.

Nevertheless, this last stretch of Canterbury's defensive moat was
destroyed in 1969, when the second stage of the city's ring road was
constructed.

(Fisk-Moore)

Another Fisk-Moore view of the Dane John Moat, but with a much clearer view of the medieval city wall, and the D-shaped bastions along this stretch. In all, there were twenty-four defensive towers or bastions situated around the city wall circuit. They were built between the end of the 14th and late 15th centuries, sometimes at a later date than the city wall against which they abutted. Of the twenty-four medieval bastions originally built, thirteen still survive in more or less their original state, and three more which have been extensively altered. The four D-shaped, or horse-shoe shaped, bastions along the moat between Worthgate and Riding Gate are amongst those still in their original state. However, the actual city wall between these bastions was re-faced and raised in height during the 19th century.

(Fisk-Moore)

This old advertisement comes from the 1924 official guide to Canterbury, as do a number of others featured in this book. The photograph was taken from the Dane John mound and looks through the mid-point break in the famous avenue of lime trees, towards the large Georgian house, now a private hotel. By the 1930s Mrs Francis' hotel had become the municipal buildings. They remained as such until the early 1980s, when the new municipal buildings were constructed along Military Road. The Dane John Gardens were created in the 1790s by Alderman James Simmons and have changed very little in their two hundred year existence. The old municipal buildings have come full circle and are now once again private residences.

Many fine late Georgian houses can be found around the north west perimeter of the Dane John Gardens (of course, the city wall rampart runs along the south east perimeter). This 1941 picture shows the early nineteenth century terraced houses at Nos. 1 to 7 Dane John, with the rather neglected gardens in the foreground.

The house furthest from the camera (No. 1) was the premises of Albert Bright, the shops act inspector. This end property was destroyed in the October 1942 raid, together with some adjoining properties in Watling Street. The surviving properties were threatened with demolition in the mid 1960s, to make way for the council's grandiose civic centre scheme. Fortunately, this plan was subsequently cancelled.

(Fisk-Moore, Courtesy Canterbury Museums)

(Above) The 'new' Kent and Canterbury Hospital was opened in 1937 on 8½ acres of land in South Canterbury. This view is looking north. It is a fine example of the art-deco or 'moderne' style of architecture, popular at the time but uncommon in Canterbury. Note the Elham Valley railway line in the foreground, and the hospital driveway, before the horse-chestnut trees were planted.

(Kent Messenger)

(Below) The old Kent and Canterbury Hospital is visible in the centre of this 1932 view. However, of special interest is St George's Place running across the bottom half of the picture. The long terrace of elegant three-storey buildings can clearly be seen on the street's north side. This view also pre-dates the construction of the Regal Cinema (now the Cannon), also in St George's Place.

(Kentish Gazette)

(Above) Cityscape looking north-west. The lost buildings of Lower Chantry Lane, including the Payne-Smith School, are visible in the bottom half of the picture. Also of special note are the Star brewery buildings against the city wall in Broad Street. Abbotts Mill in St Radigund's Street can just be seen in the top left hand corner of the picture, and the Northgate suburbs in the top right.

(Kentish Gazette)

(Below) The Longport and St Martin's area on the north-east outskirts of the city. In the centre are the Canterbury prison buildings, with St Martin's Church on the right. Note the lost cottages along St Martin's Hill and the, as yet, undeveloped North Holmes Road area. The green area north of the prison is now occupied by Christ Church College.

(Kentish Gazette)

OLD DOVER ROAD

It is nice to be able to feature a pre-war picture of a building that can still be seen in Canterbury today, unlike so many others either lost in the blitz or demolished in the 1960s. The photograph was taken in the late 1930s by the Kent Messenger and shows the St Mary Bredin Vicarage at No. 18 Old Dover Road. At this time, the resident was the Reverend John Lewis who had been the vicar of St Mary Bredin Church since 1931. The church itself was roughly half a mile away in Rose Lane.

The parish of St Mary Bredin purchased this building to be their new vicarage around 1882. On the 3rd, 4th and 5th October of that year a 'Grande Bazaar' was held in the Corn Exchange to raise funds for this venture.

The vicarage survived the blitz of Canterbury, unlike the church of St Mary Bredin which was destroyed by fire. Subsequently, a new church was built in 1957, only a few hundred yards away from the vicarage, on the opposite side of the Old Dover Road.

In 1965 the old vicarage was threatened with demolition, to make way for an office block development. Fortunately, planning permission was refused on the grounds that the old building was 'of special architectural interest and an essential feature in the street picture of Old Dover Road'.

In the event, the developers got their way, and just built round the old vicarage. Today it is surrounded closely by modern office blocks, containing the National Westminster Bank and County Court.

Inevitably, the old vicarage itself is now an office building.

(Kent Messenger)

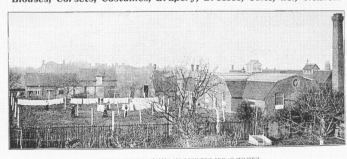

Old Dover Road is a very ancient thoroughfare and once formed part of the famous Roman Watling Street. This view shows the lovely Jacobean influenced house on the south side of Old Dover Road, known as The Hoystings. In 1940, when the photograph was taken, the house was numbered 92 and owned by a Mrs Walsh.

In medieval times this particular area was a chalk quarry from which large amounts of building material for foundations were extracted. Many of Canterbury's ancient walls and buildings were constructed on chalk blocks.

The Hoystings survived the blitz of Canterbury. It has since been re-numbered 56, stripped of all creepers, divided into flats and extended to the end nearest the camera.

(Kent Messenger)

Oaten Hill is a short stretch of road running north from its junction with Old Dover Road to a point just a hundred yards away. Here the road splits to become Dover Street and Upper Chantry Lane. The name Oaten probably comes from the existence of a medieval oat market held here, and Hill from a small Roman burial mound that once stood where the road splits.

The photograph shows the building on the corner of Oaten Hill with Old Dover Road. Much of the property is taken up by the Cross Keys public house at No. 24 Oaten Hill. The smaller premises on the left belongs to Leslie Welch, a bakers shop with the address of No. 19 Old Dover Road.

Today the pub takes up the entire building.

(Kent Messenger)

Because of the enormity of the Baedeker raid of 1st June 1942 and the loss of both life and buildings, the earlier minor raids of 1940 tend to become overshadowed or completely forgotten. The 'hit and run' raid of October 1940 that caused damage in Burgate Street is relatively well known (see page 59), but the first raid to cause actual loss of life in Canterbury occurred on 27th August 1940. A single enemy aircraft dropped three high explosive bombs which destroyed seven houses in Cossington Road, off Oaten Hill. Regrettably, four people were killed and many others buried alive in the rubble of their former homes.

This picture was taken in 1941 and looks across the devastation in Cossington Road. The 'new' Telephone House building of 1939 can be seen in the distance.

(Rob Williams)

ST GEORGE'S PLACE

The old photograph, which dates from the late 1930s, shows part of the elegant terrace on the north side of St George's Place, locally referred to as 'doctors row'. The centrepiece was the house of Dr Wacher at No. 9 St George's Place, with the gable end. The house was also notable for a huge wisteria which completely covered and hung from the first floor balcony.

Taking the whole terrace from left to right: at No. 5 is the surgery of Doctors Stevens and Freshman. No. 6 St George's Place contained Elise Ltd, gowns and sportswear shop, and No. 7, the photographic studio of B. & W. Fisk-Moore. No. 8 was the house of Dr Willis, but in the mid 30s had become Jeneel's hairdresser. All these properties had separate residential accommodation on the upper floors.

No. 10 St George's Place had also been a doctor's house, that of Dr Ferguson, but by the time the photograph was taken had been occupied by the Alliance Assurance Co. Ltd and the County Fire Office Ltd. Each house in the row had a substantial cellar and some, including No. 9, had a rear garage that could by accessed from Ivy Lane behind.

The entire 'doctors row' was destroyed by fire in the blitz of Canterbury. Dr Wacher's house was completely gutted and had almost entirely collapsed, although the cellar and many of its contents had incredibly escaped destruction.

Today the premises of the Kentish Gazette stands on the site of Dr Wacher's house, and is also No. 9 St George's Place. And what is more, the old garage once to the rear of the house still survives, and is used by the Gazette as a storeroom.

(Kent Messenger)

The late Georgian terrace of houses on the north side of St George's Place continued along to the junction with Lower Chantry Lane. This view shows some of those houses, which by the late 1930s had been taken over by various insurance companies and estate agents! (Unfortunately, in Canterbury today, former houses are still being converted into offices.) On the left of the picture is the tobacconist and confectionery shop of Edward Ralph.

The fires of the Baedeker raid reduced these buildings to fragile charred shells which were quickly demolished within weeks of the blitz. In the immediately post-war years a petrol filling station and car park could be found here. Today Safeways supermarket and a second carriageway for St George's Place occupy the site.

(Kent Messenger)

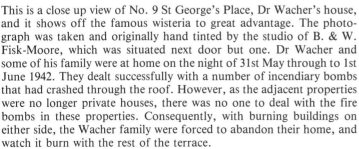

This is a close up view of No. 9 St George's Place, Dr Wacher's house, and it shows off the famous wisteria to great advantage. The photograph was taken and originally hand tinted by the studio of B. & W. Fisk-Moore, which was situated next door but one. Dr Wacher and some of his family were at home on the night of 31st May through to 1st June 1942. They dealt successfully with a number of incendiary bombs that had crashed through the roof. However, as the adjacent properties were no longer private houses, there was no one to deal with the fire bombs in these properties. Consequently, with burning buildings on either side, the Wacher family were forced to abandon their home, and watch it burn with the rest of the terrace.

(Fisk-Moore)

As the name implies, New Dover Road is not one of Canterbury's most ancient thoroughfares. It was constructed about 1790 and, together with St George's Place, formed a new toll road for London to Dover coaching traffic. This impressive four-storey building on the corner of Lower Chantry Lane and New Dover Road was built in the early 1800s, at the same time as much of St George's Place. At the time this picture was taken in 1940 the corner building played host to several firms of chartered accountants and also contained the premises of the Canterbury Citizens Advice Bureau. Unfortunately, it was completely destroyed in the Canterbury blitz as were many other buildings in nearby St George's Place and Lower Chantry Lane. In the late 1950s the empty site was purchased by Caffyns for the construction of a new commercial vehicle and stores building.

(Kent Messenger)

47

LOWER CHANTRY LANE

Before the blitz of Canterbury Lower Chantry Lane contained some thirty-one dwelling houses. Apart from Chantry House, a large detached Georgian building, the remaining thirty houses were small and arranged in four terraces. One terrace was at the top end of the lane, situated between the junction with St George's Place and Chantry House. The other three were towards the bottom, or Longport end, of Lower Chantry Lane.

This Kent Messenger picture dates from 1941, and features two of those rows of cottages. Nearest the camera is the terrace at Nos. 11 to 18 Chantry Lane. They were situated between the extensive garden of Chantry House and the junction with Ivy Lane. These houses were damaged in the June 1942 raids, but were finally destroyed on 31st January 1944, when an enemy Junkers 88 bomber aircraft crashed onto Lower Chantry Lane.

The other terrace at Nos. 28 to 37 can be seen further down the lane on the other side. They were destroyed in the 1st June 1942 blitz. The Payne-Smith School, opposite these particular houses, was also a victim of the same raid.

The final terrace of small houses, the Coopers almshouses, are just out of sight on the right of the photograph. They survived the Second World War and are currently the only six houses in Lower Chantry Lane. However, the recently published Canterbury District Plan identifies two areas in the lane for residential use. Both sites are currently small surface car parks. The large coach park at the bottom end of the lane, and visible in the current picture, is to become a coach setting down/picking up point, as well as providing parking for all the new residents of Lower Chantry Lane.

(Kent Messenger)

KENT & CANTERBURY HOSPITAL.
(Founded 1793).

President: The Right Hon. Lord Northbourne.
Chairman: Bernard H. Holland, Esq., C.B.

For the year 1923 the following cases were treated:—
In-patients admitted, 1,483. Out-patients 21,918.
Permanent Income from Invested Funds
approximate £2,200.

£11,000

is required each year to meet the Deficit. Friends of the Hospital are kindly asked for their generous support towards obtaining this sum each year. Contributions may be sent to the Secretary of the Hospital Propaganda Committee, 62 Burgate Street, Canterbury, or to the Secretary of the Hospital, Longport Canterbury.

There was a terrace of small cottages adjacent to Chantry House that were numbered 4 to 9 Lower Chantry Lane. They are pictured here in a postcard view from the 1920s. The cottage at No. 4 nearest the camera was one of the contenders for the title 'Uriah Heep's 'Umble 'ome' (see also page 5). Chantry House and its garden wall can also be seen here.
(Courtesy Derek Butler)

This large 18th century building is Chantry House at No. 10 Lower Chantry Lane. It was situated halfway between the junctions with St George's Place and Ivy Lane. According to a pre-war Ordnance Survey map of Canterbury, the house and its grounds occupied the site of the original Doges Chantry. However, the late Dr William Urry favoured a site on the other side of the lane, adjacent to today's Edward Road. Regrettably Chantry House was yet another victim of the bombing. Shortly after the war the Inland Revenue moved onto the site of the house, in a series of prefabricated buildings. At this time sections of the substantial garden wall of Chantry House remained, but these last traces were removed when Lower Chantry Lane was widened to its present size in 1956. Today Safeway supermarket occupies the site of Chantry House and its garden.

(Kent Messenger)

This picture was taken from near the junction with Longport, and looks back up Lower Chantry Lane. The cottages seen here at Nos. 28 to 37 are also visible in the view on page 48. In the immediate foreground are the wooden fence and gates of the premises of E. Crouch and Sons, plumbers. Beyond the cottages the smaller Cooper Almshouses are just visible.

(Kent Messenger)

Lower Chantry Lane leads into Longport, a much wider thoroughfare that runs along the southern boundary of the old St Augustine's Monastery. A left turn into Longport would have taken you past the Kent and Canterbury Hospital, and into Monastery Street. Then, coming off this latter street was Church Street St Paul's (pages 50 and 51) and finally Lady Wootton's Green (pages 52 and 53). Returning to the Longport junction, a right turn would have immediately led you past the cottages in this picture. They were numbered 30 to 34 and situated on the south side of Longport between the aforementioned junction and the entrance to the remote St Paul's burial ground. The cottages were blitz victims, and today the site is occupied by an improved junction into Lower Chantry Lane, and public conveniences.

(Fisk-Moore, Courtesy Canterbury Museums)

CHURCH STREET ST PAUL'S

Church Street St Paul's is an ancient thoroughfare that existed as far back as Roman times. Then it formed the beginning of the road out of Canterbury that ultimately led to the sea port of Richborough. In Saxon times a chapel dedicated to St Paul may have existed on the site of today's church.

The old picture was taken by Fisk-Moore in the winter of 1940-41 and features many of the impressive buildings which could be found along the north side of Church Street St Paul's.

The large Georgian building on the left is the premises of J.G. Cleaver Ltd; Valuers at No. 5. Next to this is a private dwelling, and beyond that an older timber framed building at No. 7 Church Street St Paul's. This housed the tea rooms run by Mr Edward Middleton, as well as the headquarters of the Canterbury Labour Party (Keir Hardie Hall). Beyond are further private residences at Nos. 8 to 12.

Many of these buildings perished in the blitz of Canterbury, but the three large houses at Nos. 9 to 11 Church Street survived and can be seen in the current picture. On the right of both photographs can be seen St Paul's Church. This has been rebuilt a number of times during its long existence as a place of worship. It survived the blitz intact, but the adjacent small church hall was destroyed.

Also common to both views is the old cemetery gate, once belonging to St Augustine's Abbey. Built in 1390, the gate was converted into a private dwelling in 1839.

(Fisk-Moore, Courtesy Canterbury Museums)

This slightly earlier view of Church Street shows the south side, which is dominated by St Paul's Church. As mentioned opposite, a Saxon chapel with the same dedication may have once stood here, but so far no remains have been traced. The present church originates from the early 13th century, but has since been substantially enlarged twice. On the first occasion, in the late 14th century, the church was extended eastwards to draw level with the 13th century tower. The second and most extensive enlargement started in 1847 when the church was extended to the south by the addition of a new aisle and choir vestry. The tower's roof and many of the replacement windows in the medieval body of the church are also 19th century.

(Courtesy Derek Butler)

The 19th century enlargement of St Paul's Church was carried out under the auspices of William John Chesshyre, vicar of this parish from 1842 until his death in 1859. Other achievements under his leadership include the establishment of the National Schools in Broad Street and the St Paul's Infant School. The infant school buildings were situated behind the church and were constructed of flint. Part of St Paul's Infant School is pictured here, with the church being situated immediately behind the cameraman. The school hall was situated to the side of the church and can be seen in the top picture. The hall was destroyed in the blitz and replaced by a prefabricated building which survives today. However, the main school buildings behind the church have since been demolished.

(Fisk-Moore)

This photograph shows the large building that once stood on the corner of Church Street St Paul's with Monastery Street. Like many of the other houses on the north side of Church Street, it dates from the late 18th or early 19th century. This was a period when late Georgian buildings were constructed over much of this part of Canterbury. As can clearly be seen, the building encompassed the Monastery Coffee Tavern and St Paul's Young Men's Club. By the late 1930s the property had been divided into two; as a private residence at No. 12 Church Street, and as a Doctors Surgery (Bailey House) at No. 1 Monastery Street. The entire building was destroyed in the blitz. Today the still undeveloped corner site is laid out as a seating area.

(Courtesy Canterbury Museums)

LADY WOOTTON'S GREEN

Lady Wootton's Green is a short and attractive thoroughfare that links Broad Street and Monastery Street. It takes its name from Lady Wootton, the wife of a 17th century Lord Lieutenant of Kent. They lived in the nearby St Augustine Palace, which was largely made up of buildings from the former St Augustine's Abbey. Before Lord and Lady Wootton's time, the thoroughfare was known as Mulberry Tree Green.

Before the Second World War, Lady Wootton's Green was even more attractive than it is today, as it contained many fine old buildings. This Kent Messenger picture dates from 1940 and features three ancient cottages that could once be found on the green's north side. Numbered 2 to 4, they were situated between the passages through to The Almonery and Mount Pleasant. No. 4 furthest from the camera is timber framed and may have been medieval. The other two cottages are brick built and of later construction.

Abbott Findon's Great Gate of 1309, which once formed part of St Augustine's Abbey, can also be seen in this view. After the dissolution of 1538 most of the abbey church was demolished. However, the Findon Gate survived as it became part of the aforementioned royal palace. In fact all of the buildings that survived from the old abbey did so because they were re-used as part of the palace.

The gate was badly blast damaged in the blitz of Canterbury, but was subsequently restored. The cottages, however, were destroyed. Two very attractive timber framed buildings on the south side of Lady Wootton's Green were also victims of the bombing.

(Kent Messenger)

Another view of the same cottages on page 52 but taken from the Findon Gate and looking back towards Broad Street. This picture also features the large house at No. 1 Lady Wootton's Green, the roof of which can be seen beyond the cottages. This was the only house to escape destruction in the bombing of 1st June 1942, although it received severe blast damage. One of the cottages, No. 2 furthest from the camera, also escaped destruction. However, it was so badly damaged that a decision was made not to retain it. In the 1950s Monastery Street was extended through to link up with Havelock Street. The new road was built to the left of the old archway seen in the picture, and through where the blitzed cottages had once stood.

(Fisk-Moore, Courtesy Canterbury Museums)

Canterbury has a wealth of timber framed secular buildings which have survived from the medieval period. They can mainly be found within the city walls or along the old routes into the city such as in St Dunstan's Street, Northgate, Dover Street or Wincheap. There was also a concentration of them in the area between the city wall and the extra-mural religious houses of St Augustine's Abbey and St Gregory's Priory. Regrettably, many of the old timber framed houses in this area became victims of the blitz. One such lost building was this fine house on the south side of Lady Wootton's Green, near the junction with Monastery Street. At a later date, the building appears to have been altered and possibly extended using bricks at the far end. Furthermore, the roof at that end of the house does not look original.

(Kent Messenger)

This and the photograph above both come from the archives of the Kent Messenger and were taken in 1941. The fine timber framed buildings along the south side of Lady Wootton's Green can be seen to good advantage. The houses in the foreground demonstrate the advanced pattern of timber framing achieved by the 17th century. Moreover, with their jettied gables, they are typical of a number of such buildings found in Canterbury. In many cases these larger post-medieval houses replaced earlier medieval timber-framed dwellings on the same site.

High explosive bombs caused the destruction of many properties in the vicinity of St Augustine's Abbey, including those seen here. Together, the pictures on this page show just what an attractive place pre-war Lady Wootton's Green was.

(Kent Messenger)

BROAD STREET

Broad Street closely follows Canterbury's city wall round from Northgate to Burgate, a distance representing just under 20% of its circumference. Originally the defensive ditch or moat lay between Broad Street and the wall, but this was eventually filled in and developed. The other side of the street had been completely developed in medieval times, despite being outside of the city walls, and many of these ancient buildings survived until the blitz of Canterbury.

This old Fisk-Moore photograph was taken near the junction with Lady Wootton's Green, and clearly shows how Broad Street got its name. The old house on the right of the picture stands at that junction, and was known as The Priory. It was reputed to be the house wherein Charles Dickens wrote 'David Copperfield'. Sometime between the world wars this house had been modernised and many old features removed.

The more humble mixed terrace seen along Broad Street contained eleven dwellings between The Priory and The Brewers Delight public house. The pub is the white building furthest from the camera. Some of the medieval buildings that had survived until this time can be seen along this stretch, although most of the houses are from the early to mid 19th century. Nevertheless, every building in this picture, with the exception of The Brewers Delight, was lost as a result of the 1942 bombing.

Diocesan House was subsequently built on the site of The Priory and old people's bungalows replaced the terraced houses. The Brewers Delight public house can still be found in Broad Street today.

(Fisk-Moore, Courtesy Canterbury Museums)

This is a much earlier view of The Priory and shows the complete elevation of the house facing Lady Wootton's Green. As mentioned opposite, the house was 'modernised' between the world wars. Compare this picture with the later view to see that many of the old windows were replaced, the chimney stack shortened, and the garden shrubs taken out.

(H.B. Collis)

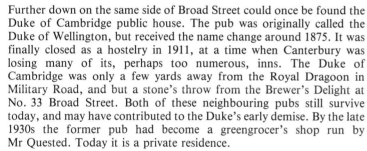

Further down on the same side of Broad Street could once be found the Duke of Cambridge public house. The pub was originally called the Duke of Wellington, but received the name change around 1875. It was finally closed as a hostelry in 1911, at a time when Canterbury was losing many of its, perhaps too numerous, inns. The Duke of Cambridge was only a few yards away from the Royal Dragoon in Military Road, and but a stone's throw from the Brewer's Delight at No. 33 Broad Street. Both of these neighbouring pubs still survive today, and may have contributed to the Duke's early demise. By the late 1930s the former pub had become a greengrocer's shop run by Mr Quested. Today it is a private residence.

A further view of the section of Broad Street featured in the picture on the opposite page. It dates from 1941 and was taken from Broad Street car park. The Priory received a direct hit in the Baedeker raid, and was totally destroyed. The other cottages in this photograph were blast damaged and later cleared away, being considered beyond repair.

(Rob Williams)

This photograph shows another section of Broad Street, this time south of the junction with Lady Wootton's Green. It features perhaps an even more fascinating row of houses and shops, many of which are timber framed and probably medieval in date. In fact, they are shown on Braun and Hogenberg's map of Canterbury, published in the late 16th century. The brick building on the left, of more recent construction, is the premises of Sydney Orton — electrical engineer. Next door is the much older antique shop run by Mr Todd. These two premises were still standing after the main June blitz, but like many similar blast damaged buildings were only considered fit for demolition. The properties further up Broad Street at Nos. 8 to 10 did survive and can be seen today.

(Rob Williams)

BURGATE STREET

Wartime destruction in St George's Street was almost 100% with only Marks and Spencer surviving intact. In Burgate Street blitz damage was less severe, but even here around half of its buildings were destroyed.

The old pre-war photograph shows the lost buildings on either side of the Canterbury Lane junction, as well as some impressive ones in Burgate Street itself which have survived to this day.

The large three-storey building on the left, with the neo-classical doorway, was the Kent & Canterbury Hospital's private nurses' institute, with Miss Purchas as matron. To the right, at No. 61 Burgate Street, is a smaller scale three-storey building which was the premises of Fielding and Pembrook Solicitors, and the registered office of Shelford Brickworks Ltd.

On the other side of Canterbury Lane is the Canterbury dispensary which had a resident medical officer. This building was relatively new when the picture was taken, and had replaced a previous timber framed dispensary building. On the far right is the presbytery of St Thomas Catholic Church at No. 59 Burgate Street, with the church itself next door and just out of the picture.

The solicitors' building and the dispensary were destroyed by fire in the blitz of Canterbury, which had swept along the lanes of the old St George's parish.

Post-war reconstruction of Canterbury Lane and the south side of Burgate Street finally occurred in the mid to late 1950s. An extension to the Catholic Presbytery subsequently appeared on the site of the old dispensary, and a row of rather austere shops was built in 1959 on the east side of a now wider Canterbury Lane.

(Fisk-Moore, Courtesy of Canterbury Museums)

This is an earlier photograph than the one opposite and gives a better view of the smaller three-storey buildings at No. 61 Burgate Street. In the late 1930s it had become a solicitors' office, but appeared still to be a private residence in this older view. The Reverend Richard Harris Barham was born in this house on 6th December 1788. Better known as 'Thomas Ingoldsby', he was responsible for the many short stories and poems, collectively called 'The Ingoldsby Legends'.

On the other side of Canterbury Lane can be seen the original timber framed dispensary building, later to be replaced by the one seen on page 56. St Thomas' Church presbytery and St Mary Magdalene Tower can be seen further along Burgate Street.

(Kentish Gazette)

Court Brothers Ltd owned a number of shops in pre-war Burgate Street. Apart from the properties on the south side of the street (see below), they also owned this large imposing shop at No. 24 on the north side of Burgate Street. It is pictured here as part of an advertisement that first appeared in the 1903 guide to Canterbury.

Although much of Court Bros shop premises in Burgate Street was lost in the blitz, this particular shop survived. It can be seen today, although under different ownership. There is a certain cruel irony in the fact that the only part of their premises on the south side of the street to have survived the war was destroyed by fire in 1956.

In amongst the shops of Burgate Street could be found the old rear entrance gateway into the Longmarket and Corn Exchange building. This small neo-classical structure was built in 1824 and contained public conveniences on each side. It was constructed of red brick with a Stucco finish, as was the main Corn Exchange frontage facing onto St George's Street (see page 25). Once through the gateway, there was a covered passageway which led into the building proper. The shops just visible on either side of the gate both belong to Court Brothers Ltd, the house furnishers. Both shops were lost in the blitz of Canterbury, but the gateway survived. It was eventually demolished in two stages, in 1956 and 1958 (see 'Canterbury Then and Now' pages 8 and 9).

(Kent Messenger)

THE LANES

The old street pattern of Canterbury included a number of narrow lanes running in a north-south direction and interlinking the larger and more important cross-city thoroughfares. Most survive today in name, but the vast majority have been either blitzed or demolished; then widened and rebuilt to be unrecognisable from their sleepy pre-war appearance.

Iron Bar Lane was one such tiny narrow lane, and is pictured here looking northwards towards its junction with Burgate Street. It was a ramshackle collection of timber framed and brick buildings which mixed private dwellings and business premises. For example, on the east side in 1937 could be found the premises of Percy Maple, bookbinder, and C. Lee, furniture stores, as well as the tiny cottages of Mrs Corrigan and Mrs Curtis. The western side contained the depository of Godden & Son and the small tailors shop of William A. Dean.

The Crown Inn stood on the eastern corner of Iron Bar Lane with Burgate Street, and can be seen at the end of the terrace in the old photograph. This ancient public house, reputed to have dated from the 15th century, was badly damaged in the minor hit and run raids on Canterbury in the autumn of 1940. It continued to trade with much of the first storey gone, only to be completely destroyed in the Baedeker raid of June 1942. In fact, every single building in Iron Bar Lane was razed to the ground on that terrible night. Today Iron Bar Lane can only be accessed from St George's Street on foot, and the much widened stretch from Burgate Street leads to a small parking area. The Lane's post-war buildings are of little architectural merit.

(Courtesy Derek Butler)

Butchery Lane runs parallel to, and west of, Iron Bar Lane. In the pre-war years it was less humble than Iron Bar Lane and contained shops and public houses on both sides. This picture was taken from half way along Butchery Lane and looks north towards Burgate Street. Along the west side, as today, could be found the City Arms and Shakespeare public houses, whilst on the east side was another pub known as the Butcher's Arms.

Approximately two-thirds of the eastern side of Butchery Lane, including the pub, was lost in the blitz. The remaining third was gradually whittled away between 1947 and 1959.

The west side of the lane survived the war completely intact.

(Courtesy Derek Butler)

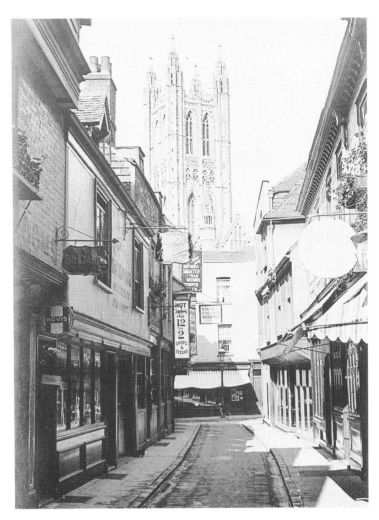

Another photograph of Iron Bar Lane, but taken in the opposite direction, that is from the Burgate Street junction and looking south along the lane. The Crown Inn public house can be seen here in this 1941 view, showing the damage sustained in the minor raid from the previous year. Much of the first storey was lost but, as can be seen in the picture, a temporary corrugated iron roof was fashioned and trade continued. The Crown Inn was finally completely destroyed by fire in the Baedeker raid of June 1942. The undamaged building just visible on the left is the premises of antique dealer, Mrs Lucy Lee. It abutted directly onto the old St Mary Magdalene Church tower, and was another victim of the June 1942 blitz.

(Fisk-Moore, Courtesy Canterbury Museums)

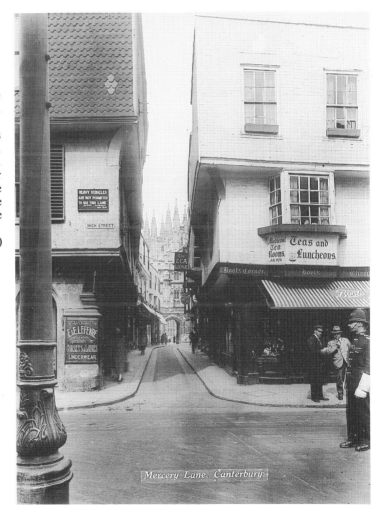

Grander still than both Iron Bar Lane and Butchery Lane is Mercery Lane, the most famous and often photographed lane in Canterbury. This picture was taken between the world wars, but differs very little from the same view today. A surviving range of the Chequers of Hope Inn runs along the lanes west (left) side (see page 15). The east side also has many fine old buildings, including the premises of Boots the chemist in the foreground. Although the basic structure of this building is medieval, its external appearance has been much altered in the last hundred years to seem even more 'old-fashioned'. The survival of Mercery Lane is a clear reminder that the blitz of Canterbury, although terrible, could have been a lot worse.

(Fisk-Moore)

59

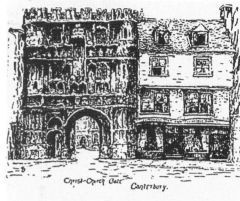

CHRIST CHURCH GATE

Christ Church Gate was the last great construction project associated with the Cathedral to be undertaken before the Reformation. The gate was probably built sometime between 1505 and 1520, and immediately followed the construction of Bell Harry Tower. They actually share the main method of construction in being made of stone in the lower section and Tudor red brick above faced with stone, to reduce the overall weight of the structure.

When new, Christ Church Gate appeared very much as it does today, but much has happened to its fabric in the intervening years. For example, in 1643, during the civil war, parliamentary troops tore down the statue of Christ from the niche above the entrance arch and burned the large wooden doors. The present doors are replacements and date from 1660.

Then around 1800 the gate's twin turrets were dismantled at the request of Alderman James Simmons so that he could see the Cathedral clock from his bank premises on the corner of St Margaret's Street and High Street (now Lloyds Bank). At about the same time the remaining fabric of the gate was 'restored' when much of the exterior was re-faced. Nevertheless, by 1900, around which time the old photograph was taken, Christ Church Gate looked in a very sorry state with much of the detail eroded away.

Proper restoration began in 1931 and was undertaken by the Friends of the Cathedral. The twin turrets were rebuilt in 1937, and finally, in the recent past, a lovely statue of Christ was restored to the niche above the entrance that had previously been empty for around 350 years.

Today Christ Church Gate must surely be one of the most photographed buildings in Canterbury.

(H.B. Collis)

In front of Christ Church Gate is an open area known as the Buttermarket, surrounded by medieval buildings. Burgate Street, Mercery Lane and Sun Street all converge at the Buttermarket. This very early picture probably dates from about 1888, the year when the Buttermarket's covered building, with its iron columns and wooden dome, was removed. Shortly afterwards, a memorial to Christopher Marlowe was erected in the centre of the Buttermarket. This attractive statue of a semi-naked muse was moved to the Dane John Gardens in 1921, where it can be found today. It was replaced on the market site by the present First World War memorial. Today in summer the Buttermarket is a hive of activity.

This early postcard view of Christ Church Gate was probably taken at around the same time as the photograph opposite. However, this much closer view of the lower part of the gate shows just how badly the stone facing had deteriorated. The wooden doors of 1660 can also clearly be seen, and appear to be in much better condition than the stonework. The restoration work begun in 1931 took four years to complete. The front cover photograph from 1932 shows the structure covered in scaffolding, with the work clearly in progress. The then Cathedral architect, Mr W.D. Caroe, was responsible for the restoration work, and the cost was met by the Friends of Canterbury Cathedral.

(H.B. Collis)

Before passing through Christ Church Gateway, nearby Sun Street is worth a look, particularly the late medieval Sun Hotel. It has often been photographed, not only because of its fine double-jettied timber framing, but also because it featured in 'David Copperfield', but was called therein the 'Little Inn'. Until the early 19th century all incoming coaching traffic from the Sturry Road would have passed by the hotel. However, Sun Street proved too narrow, so Guildhall Street was created for more easy passage into the heart of the city. Fortunately, the Sun Hotel survived the great fire of 1865 that destroyed so many of the ancient timber framed buildings in the Sun Street, Guildhall Street, High Street and Mercery Lane block.

(Fisk-Moore)

CANTERBURY CATHEDRAL

In the four hundred years that separated the Reformation and the start of Queen Victoria's reign, very little repair or renovation work was carried out on the fabric of the Cathedral (the destruction of Lanfranc's north-west tower was a notable and regrettable exception). In fact many of the redundant monastic buildings of the former Christ Church Priory were allowed to fall into ruin, or dismantled for building materials.

The old photograph dates from the 1920s, and shows the old monastic cloisters in a very sorry state of disrepair. Fortunately, extensive restoration work has since been carried out, and the beautiful perpendicular stonework is now a splendid sight, as the current picture illustrates.

There are a number of other notable differences between the old and current views. The Victorian library with its round western window can be seen to the right of the old photograph. It was built in 1868 amongst the ruins of Archbishop Lanfranc's monastic dormitory. Part of the old dormitory, dating from 1080, can be seen between the cloisters and the library. This arcade of round-topped arches, some with window openings and some blind, once extended round the entire upper storey of the dormitory building.

The story of the Cathedral's miraculous escape from serious blitz damage is now well known. However, the Victorian library received a direct hit and was almost completely destroyed. Fortunately, the ancient section of Lanfranc's dormitory wall arcade survived, and was incorporated into the new library, the construction of which was completed in 1954.

Other changes include the removal of the upright tombstones from the garth, and the felling of many trees in the garden beyond.

(Fisk-Moore)

The Visitor, having been shown over the Cathedral, should walk round the edifice through the Dark Entry to the Green Court where may be seen in the far corner the famous Norman Staircase, and passing under the archway of the King's School, a fine view is obtained through the gateway of one of the oldest houses in Canterbury, presented as part endowment of Jesus' Hospital in 1583 by Sir Jon Boys; now known as

YE OLDE CURIOSITIE TEA SHOPPE.

28 Palace Street, where nice refreshments may be obtained at a very moderate price. :: Visitors recommended.

Journey's end for all pilgrims to Canterbury, the magnificent Cathedral, seen here in 1935 from an upper chamber of Christ Church Gate. The entire west end of the Cathedral, including the three main towers and nave seen here, is all built in the perpendicular Gothic style. They replaced earlier Norman or Romanesque work in gradual stages. First to be rebuilt was the nave from 1377 to 1405. At this time, the lofty new perpendicular nave must have looked strange, sandwiched between the three original Norman towers. Next was the south-west tower (nearest the camera) rebuilt from 1424 to 1434, and then Bell Harry Tower from 1494 to 1503. The old Romanesque north-west tower lingered on until 1832, when it was finally replaced by a matching copy of the south-west tower.

(Fisk-Moore)

As stated on the page opposite, after the dissolution of Christ Church Priory in 1540 those of its buildings not absorbed by the Dean and Chapter, or the new King's School, were allowed to fall into ruin. One such former monastic building was the infirmary to the north of the Corona Tower. The old picture shows the remaining row of arches and the west end of the infirmary hall, both dating from the early 12th century. After the old infirmary had become ruinous, houses were constructed against the surviving arches. However, these were all demolished in the last century. In 1966 the red bricked Wolfson Library was built above the old dark entry, and partly sits on top of the old west wall of the infirmary.

(Fisk-Moore)

Leaving the Cathedral by the dark entry to the north, one has to pass through Prior Sellinger's Gatehouse, built in the 1400s. This early 1930s photograph was taken from the Green Court and looks south towards the gate, with the Cathedral dominating the background. The curious little tower seen beyond the Gatehouse and to the left was once part of the monastic chequer building or counting house. This tower now adjoins the aforementioned new Wolfson Library. Prior Sellinger's Gatehouse has been restored in recent years and ivy is no longer allowed to cling to its walls. The large tree on the Green Court to the right of the view is also a thing of the past. Around the Green Court, and mostly behind the cameraman, are other ex-monastic buildings which are now part of the King's School.

(Fisk-Moore)

(Above) A closer and slightly later view than the one on page 43. The Star brewery has given way to the Broad Street car park, opened in 1931. In fact, the line of the city wall can be followed round the entire length of Broad Street. The lost buildings of Church Street St Paul's, Broad Street and Lady Wootton's Green can be seen in the foreground. Burgate Street is on the left of the picture.

(Kentish Gazette)

(Below) The magnificent Christ Church Cathedral of Canterbury, the ultimate goal of pilgrims and tourists for nearly 800 years. The lost houses in the south precincts can just be made out. Clearer are the buildings along the northside of Burgate Street and on both sides of Iron Bar Lane. Also note the Congregational Church in Guildhall Street and the many terraced houses in the St Radigund's area.

(Kentish Gazette)